A BOOK OF BALLADS

A Book of Ballads

being

The Collected Light Verse

of

A. P. HERBERT

LONDON
ERNEST BENN LIMITED

First Published in
1931

Printed
in
Great Britain

CONTENTS

LAUGHING ANN

vi CONTENTS

SHE-SHANTIES

CONTENTS

PLAIN JANE

CONTENTS

BALLADS FOR BROADBROWS

LAUGHING ANN

LAUGHING ANN

WHEN laughing Ann trips down the street
    The sun comes out as well,
The town is at her twinkling feet,
    The crier rings his bell,
The young men leap like little fish,
    Policemen stand and purr,
While husbands look behind and wish
    That they had married her.

> *Laughing Ann*
>   *Turns her head,*
> *Looks at a man*
>   *And kills him dead*
>   *With eyes that say,*
>   *" What a nice fine day!*
> *Good morning—this is Ann,*
>   *Never been kissed,*
>   *Born to be kissed,*
> *But kiss me if you can!"*

And when she steps into a shop
    The happy hosier grins,
The lordly haberdashers hop
    To furnish her with pins,
The grocer asks no other fee
    If she will glance his way,

3

And trembles while he sells her tea
To think that she must pay.

> *For laughing Ann*
>   *With innocent eyes*
> *Looks at a man*
>   *And then he dies,*
>   *With eyes that say,*
>   *"And have you, pray,*
> *Seen anything quite like Ann?*
>   *Never been kissed,*
>   *Born to be kissed,*
> *But kiss me if you can!"*

Her eyes are like two pools of wine,
  Her cheeks like roses pressed,
Her lips are full, her nose is fine,
  And you can guess the rest;
She is more pure than precious stones
  And angel is her rank,
But she has married Mr. Jones,
  The manager of the Bank

> *Ah, laughing Ann*
>   *Turns her head,*
> *Looks at a man*
>   *And kills him dead,*
>   *With eyes that say,*
>   *"Behold, I pray,*
> *This unsurpassable Ann!*
>   *But the man who owns*
>   *This jewel is Jones,*
> *So kiss me if you can!"*

So when she dances up the street
  And homeward disappears
The young men move with leaden feet,
  Policemen stand in tears,
While butchers with a vicious knife
  Assault their hateful wares,
To think that Mr. Jones's wife
  Can never now be theirs.

> *For laughing Ann*
>   *With two bright eyes*
> *Can kill a man*
>   *Of any size*
>   *With eyes that say,*
>   *" What a nice fine day!*
> *But Ann is twice as fair,*
>   *Hard to resist,*
>   *Born to be kissed,*
> *But kiss me if you dare!"*

THE SAVIOURS

SIR THINGUMMY JIG was breakfasting on bacon and
    ham and eggs,
And kidney and toast and mushrooms, and a couple
    of partridge legs,
And all the time in the *Sunday Chime*, as a baronet
    ought to do,
He studied the state of the Universe and saw that it
    was blue.

"Death!" remarked Sir Thingummy Jig. "Bring
    me a pen and ink!
Bring me a fair white writing-pad, and something
    strong to drink,
And wrap a towel about my head and don't let
    anyone in,
For I must write to *The Times* to-night, and save the
    world from sin."

But Admiral Bunkum sits in bed and quietly chews a
    roll
And sausage and mash, and marmalade, the frugal,
    manly soul.
He lights his pipe, and he reads the tripe Sir
    Thingummy wrote, and then
With a nautical cry of "Hell!" or "Hi!" he snatches
    a fountain-pen.

6

And far away in a leather chair the Duke of Doodledoo
Nibbles a rusk with a single tusk and scans the papers
   through,
And things look worse with the Universe, and the
   Admiral gives him pain,
So he rings for a young stenographer and saves the
   world again.

Civilisation seems to me to be just a trifle queer;
Rack and ruin are all around, and look at the price
   of beer!
Black with fate are the clouds to date, but if ever the
   skies are blue,
Oh, don't forget 'twas Thingummy Jig that pulled
   the nation through;
Not to speak of the Admiral and the Duke of
   Doodledoo.

MID-OCEAN; OR, THE ROVER

I'VE always been extremely keen
On anything at all marine,
  I used to rave
  About the wave
 And with no small emotion
I sometimes sang the sort of thing
That sailors are supposed to sing,
  Explaining what
  A pleasant spot
 They find the raging ocean.
But ah, how short a step is there
From high romance to *mal de mer!*
The nation, Sir, that lifts a hand
Against our well-belovèd land,
That race must reckon first with me,
But anyone can have the sea—

  Blow, breezes, blow!
  Ho (Heave, and Yo)!
  How sweet it is to roam!
  Ho (Yo, and Heave)!
  Why did I leave
  My comfortable home?

Though I am very well aware
The ocean is a grand affair

And poets who
Have seen the blue
From cosy South-Coast cities
Have sung its praises, there and then,
I can but wish these honest men

Had taken trips
In actual ships
Before they wrote their ditties.
I too have dreamed, on Brighton Pier,
A wild piratical career,
But I would sooner milk a cow
Than be a jolly pirate now.

Old England's very dear to me,
But anyone can have the sea—

> *Blow, breezes, blow!*
> *Ho (Heave, and Yo)!*
> *How bonny flies the foam!*
> *Ho (Yo, and Heave)!*
> *Why did I leave*
> *My comfortable home?*

The open sea, the open air,
The open road to anywhere,
          Are good, no doubt,
          To read about
     When one has just been dining;
But I have met no poet yet
Who saw much fun in being wet,
          Or liked to pass
          The night on grass
     Whatever stars were shining;
The very politicians yawn
If by mischance they see The DAWN,
And all adventure's spoiled for me
If I can't get my morning tea;
While I repeat with three times three
That anyone can have the sea—

> *Blow, breezes, blow!*
> *Ho (Heave, and Yo)!*
> *Across the magic foam!*
> *Ho (Yo, and Heave)!*
> *Why did I leave*
> *My comfortable home?*

EQUALITY, ETC.

SONG FOR A SOCIALIST SUNDAY SCHOOL

ALL are born equal.   Counter this who can.
  Place in his cot some scion of the rich,
Lay at his side an infant artisan,
  And who shall say for certain which is which?

> *By reason, not ruction,*
>   *We soar to the skies;*
> *The means of production*
>   *We nationalise;*
> *While rapture surprising*
>   *We bring within range*
> *By nationalising*
>   *The means of exchange.*

How comes it then that as the seasons pass
  These equal babes enjoy a different lot?
One steers the ship, one polishes the brass,
  While one is beautiful, the other not.

> *By reason, etc.*

And who can doubt that in an ordered State
  No harsh distinctions should divide the twain?
Both, hand in hand, would rule the vessel's fate,
  And both be beautiful (or both be plain).

> *By reason, etc.*

High flies the eagle; sweeter sings the wren.
  Let us be thankful, smiling through our tears,
That Heaven has made us simple honest men
  Instead of manufacturers or peers.

By reason, etc.

Yet even these we pity more than hate,
  All envious thoughts we easily subdue,
When we remember that the rich and great,
  With all their faults, are men and women too.

By reason, not ruction,
  We soar to the skies;
The means of production
  We nationalise;
While rapture surprising
  We bring within range
By nationalising
  The means of exchange.

THE RED BOX

GOOD Sir John Straight was opulent and great,
He loved his King, but he couldn't stand the
 State;
He loved his country, but he loathed her men,
And he lived in a street in W. 10.
Sir George Kildragon he dwelt there too,
And they both saw red, as the best men do—
Red for the Britisher, conqueror, chief,
Red for his blood and red for his beef,
Red across the map for the Empire's track,
And good red dollops in the Union Jack;
And when Sir John's nephew went to the War
They both saw redder than they ever saw before.

 Then ten red men came up from the Clyde,
Asked for the Parliament and walked inside,
With a funny red flag and a silly red song,
And good Sir John Straight said, "Damme! that's
 wrong."
But Sir George said, "Damme! they fought in the
 War,"
And Sir John saw redder than he ever saw before.
And Sir George he laughed at the funny red
 men,
But Sir John trotted home to W. 10;

And good Lady Straight gave him steak for a
    start,
A red rump-steak and a red plum-tart,
Red-currant jelly and a Dutch cheese (red),
With a bright red hair from the cook's red head;
And Sir John went out in a sort of a swoon,
And there in the sky was a great red moon—
Red for the Britisher, conqueror, chief,
Red for his blood and red for his beef,

"And red," said Sir John, with a strange cunning
    look,
"Red for Revolution, red for the cook,
Red for the Russians and red for the Jew,
Red for the Hospitals, red for *Who's Who*,"
And Sir John said, "Ha!" and Sir John said,
    "He!"
And Sir John said, "Ho! but you don't catch
    me."
"A *plot!*" cried Sir John Straight, standing on his
    head;
"You don't deceive *me*, Mr. Moon—you're RED!"

And that same night, in the middle of the night,
    A man put a Box,
        A Red, Red Box,
           A Scarlet Box,
                At the corner of the Street.
And Sir John said things I had better not repeat.

  Sir John fetched Sir George and they looked at the
    Box,
And Sir George said nothing, but he scratched his
    locks.
And Sir John said, " Damme, Sir, don't you see it's
    RED ?"
And Sir George said, " Damme! I've got eyes in my
    head.
It's red for the letters, John, the Red Royal Mails,
Red for King George and the little Prince of Wales,
Red for the Empire, red for the Court——"
And Sir John said rudely, " It's nothing of the
    sort.
It's the end of the wedge, Sir, that's what I allege,
It's no use a-fencing, no use to hedge—
It's red for the State, Sir, red for Bureaucracy,
Red for Interferences and red for redemocracy,
Red for the Socialists, red for the Bolshies,
Red for the Hendersons, the Webbs and the Walshes,
Moscow, Trotsky, the Third International——"
Sir George said mildly, " Come, John, be rational."
" Red," said the Baronet, foaming at the jaws,
" Red for the tumbrils, the breaking up of laws,
Red for the Empire, red for *Who's Who*,
Red for the Dutch cheese and red for the Jew.

Red in the Cabinet, the castle, the shack,
And, damme, there's a little in the *Union Jack!*
Red for the turn-coat, red for the rat,
Red for the Hospitals—and YOU TAKE THAT!"
Sir George saw redder than he previously saw,
And Sir George fetched Sir John a clipper on the jaw,
And they rolled in the road by the red, red moon,
And the red blood flowed and they both died soon—
Which generally happens when Strong Men meet
    At the Box, at the Box,
      The Red, Red Box,
        The Scarlet Box,
           At the corner of the Street.

THE INTRODUCTION; OR, TROT AWAY, MR. CLAY

Trot away, Mr. Clay—you are much in the way;
  The band, you'll observe, has begun.
There's a girl by the wall with no partner at all,
  But Miss Fish is provided with one.
There's another one there who is taken, I swear,
  With your muscular beauty and fitness,
But there's something I wish to explain to Miss Fish,
  And we shall not insist on a witness.

> *Oh, doesn't it strike you*
> *Miss Fish doesn't like you?*
>   *Away, Mr. Clay, trot away!*
> *But there's somebody here*
>   *Who is dying to meet you,*
> *She's rather a dear,*
>   *Come along—she won't eat you!*
>   *I want you to know,*
>   *Miss Amelia Blow.*
>   *This way, Mr. Clay!*
>   *Miss Blow—Mr. Clay.*
> *So glad to have seen you—Good-day.*

Trot away, Mr. Clay—in a general way
  I feel you should marry, old man,

But I'd like to explain, if you're thinking of Jane,
  You had better abandon the plan.
I am bound to report that her temper is short
  And her talk is, if anything, terser,
Her face is too fat, and, with this and with that,
  I feel you'd be wasted on her, Sir.

> *Now why don't you marry*
> *Clarissa or Carrie,*
>   *Or Poppy, or Topsy, or May?*
> *I know four or five*
>   *Who'd be only too proud,*
> *And I'll try to contrive*
>   *That you meet the whole crowd.*
>   *I want you to meet*
>   *Miss Gloria Sweet.*
>   *This way, Mr. Clay.*
>   *Miss Sweet—Mr. Clay.*
> *So glad to have seen you—Good-day.*

Trot away, Mr. Clay—in the usual way
  It is rapture to sit at your side.
To-morrow, old man, let us lunch if we can,
  Let us go for a bicycle ride.
Believe me or not, I admire you a lot,
  And in sunshine, old fellow, or stormy,
We are friends, you and I, but I cannot deny
  That just at the moment you bore me.

> *For there's something I wish*
> *To explain to Miss Fish,*
>   *And I wish you were oceans away.*

Look, there's a nice girl!
She is dying to meet you.
A pansy—a pearl,
Come along, she won't eat you!
I don't think you know
The adorable Blow.
This way, Mr. Clay!
Miss Blow—Mr. Clay.
So glad to have seen you—Good-day.

"IT MAY BE LIFE——"

I WISH I hadn't broke that dish,
   I wish I was a movie-star,
I wish a lot of things, I wish
   That life was like the movies are;

I wish I wore a wicked hat,
   I got the face for it, I *know;*
I'm tired of scrubbing floors an' that—
   It may be life, but ain't it slow?

2*

For I don't have no adventures in the street,
Men don't register emotion when we meet;
Jack don't register Love's Sweet Bliss,
Jack just registers an ordinary kiss;
> *An' I says " Evenin',"*
> *An' Jack says " Evenin',"*
> *An' we both stand there*
> *At the corner of the Square,*
Me like a statue an' him like a bear.
He don't make faces like the movie-men,
He just holds tight till the clock strikes ten,
Then I says " Friday?" an' Jack says " Right,"
Jack says " The same time?" an' I says
> *" Right;"*
Jack just whispers and I can hardly speak,
And that's the most exciting thing that happens in the
> *week.*

I'm never chased in motor-cars,
> I'm never drownded in a mine;
Them yellow men with long cigars
> Don't never ask me out to dine;
In fact, as far as I can see,
> There *is* no life in Pimlico.
Here, why don't no one kidnap *me?*
> It may be life, but ain't it slow?

> *For I don't have no adventures, etc.*

Jack loves me well enough, I know,
> But does he ever bite his lip,
And does he chew his cheek to show
> That Passion's got him in a grip?

An' does his gun go pop-pop-pop
    When fellers gets familiar?   No.
He just says, "' 'Op it!'' and they 'op—
    It may be life, but ain't it slow?

For I don't have no adventures in the street,
Men don't register emotion when we meet,

Jack don't register jealousy an' such,
Jack don't register nothing very much;
    But Jack says " Evenin',"
    An' I says " Evenin',"
    An' we both stand there
    At the corner of the Square,
  Me like a statue an' him like a bear.
He don't look loving like the movie-men,
He just holds tight till the clock strikes ten,
An' I says " Friday?" an' Jack says " Right,"

Jack says "The same time?" an' I says "Right;"

Jack just whispers and I can hardly speak,
And that's the most exciting thing that happens in the week.

An' I sometimes wish,
Oh! I very often wish
That life was a little like a movie-show;
For life may be life, but, Lordie, ain't it slow?

MY DAY OUT

HERE, Mabel, put away the joint—
    It's my day out.
It's no use arguing the point—
    It's my day out.
My Georgie's waiting in the square,
And I've my new red hat to wear,
Let's hope his mother's cut his hair,
    For it's my day out.

Oh, I likes a bit of enjoyment on a Friday,
    I never was one to scamp my work an' that,
I've laid the tea, I've left the scullery tidy,
    I've left a bit of the turbot for the cat;
I've only got to wash myself, an' it's out of this for
    Jane,
My Georgie's round the corner an' he's waiting in the
    rain,
      An' if anyone likes to ring the bell,
      Or come to the top of the stairs an' yell,
Well, I'll be snug in the pictures, dear, an' they can
ring again.

    You'd be surprised, the way we laugh
      On my day out;
    He says things fit to kill a calf
      On my day out;

An' you should see him buy the street,
I laugh till I can't hardly eat.
O Lord, I give my face a treat
    On my day out.

Oh, I likes a bit of enjoyment on a Friday,
  I like to hear the music in the parks,
I like to sit on a bus an' be the lidy,
  I like to look at the chaps an' pass remarks.
I've only got to wash myself an' it's out of this for Jane,
My Georgie's round the corner an' he's waiting in the rain,
    An' if anyone likes to ring the bell,
    Or come to the top of the stairs an' yell,
Well, I'll be snug in the pictures, dear, an' they can ring again.

It's funny how it seems to rain
    On my day out,
But there it is, we don't complain
    On my day out.
Well, if it's wet it's got to be;
It's cosy in the pictures, see?
Well, what I mean, it's him an' me
    An' my day out.

Oh, I likes a bit of enjoyment on a Friday,
  I like to sit in the fautles an' be grand,
I like to nibble an ice an' be the lidy,
  I like to sit in the dark an' hold his hand.
I've only got to wash myself an' it's out of this for Jane,

*My Georgie's round the corner an' he's waiting in the
    rain,*

       An' if anyone likes to ring the bell,

       Or come to the top of the stairs an' yell,

*Well, I'll be snug in the pictures, dear, an' they can
    ring again.*

THE PRODIGY

I KISSED my darling at the Zoo,
  And all the people snorted.
The keeper took his little book
  And said we'd be reported;

But the Small Birds sang, though a trifle flat,
And the Pelican said, " Now, fancy that!"
  In a sentimental fashion,
The Elephant sighed and went quite pale,
And the Dromedary told a tedious tale
  Of a grand but youthful passion.

The Lion no more did roar,
  And I heard the Eagles coo.
For I never had kissed my Jane before,
  And I kissed her at the Zoo.

I kissed my darling at the Zoo—
   The people left off gazing
At camel and cod and kangaroo,
   For we were more amazing;
The Octopus and the Chimpanzee
Were shocked when they looked out to see
   The usual crowd was missing,
While swarming round us, goggle-eyed,
" Ma, look at that!" the children cried,
   " Two funny creatures kissing!"

      But the Lion no more did roar,
        And I heard the Eagles coo.
      For I never had kissed my Jane before,
        And I kissed her at the Zoo.

BACON AND EGGS*

NOW blest be the Briton, his beef and his beer,
And all the strong waters that keep him in cheer,
But blest beyond cattle and blest beyond kegs
Is the brave British breakfast of bacon and eggs—

Bacon and eggs,
Bacon and eggs;
Sing bacon,
Red bacon,
Red bacon and eggs!

Thus armed and thus engined, well-shaven and gay,
We leap to our labours and conquer the day,
While paltry pale foreigners, meagre as moles,
Must crawl through the morning on coffee and rolls—

Coffee and rolls,
Barbarous rolls;
Sing coffee,
Black coffee,
Vile coffee and rolls!

What wonder the Frenchman, blown out with new
bread,
Gesticulates oft and is light in the head!

* From "King of the Castle."

31

Our perfect control of our arms and our legs
We owe to our ballast of bacon and eggs—

> *Bacon and eggs,*
> *Unemotional eggs;*
> *Sing bacon,*
> *Fat bacon,*
> *Brave bacon and eggs!*

What wonder that Fortune is careful to place
Her loveliest laurels on men of our race,
While sorrow is heaped upon Prussians and Poles
Who shame the glad morning with coffee and rolls—

> *Coffee and rolls,*
> *Ladylike rolls;*
> *Sing coffee,*
> *Pooh! coffee,*
> *Black coffee and rolls!*

What wonder the Russian looks redly because
Our England, old England, is much what it was!
We fight to the finish, we drink to the dregs
And dare to be Daniels on bacon and eggs—

> *Bacon and eggs,*
> *Masculine eggs;*
> *Sing bacon,*
> *Bring bacon,*
> *And fry me two eggs!*

But gross Europeans who constantly munch
Too little at breakfast, too freely at lunch,

Sit sated in *cafés*, incapable souls,
And go to the devil on coffee and rolls—

> *Coffee and rolls,*
> *Windy wet rolls;*
> *At coffee*
> *I'm scoffy,*
> *I execrate rolls!*

O breakfast!   O breakfast!   The meal of my heart!
Bring porridge, bring sausage, bring fish for a start,
Bring kidneys and mushrooms and partridges' legs,
But let the foundation be bacon and eggs—

> *Bacon and eggs,*
> *Bacon and eggs;*
> *Bring bacon,*
> *Crisp bacon,*
> *And let there be eggs!*

"HA!"

Major Reginald Maran
Was a Strong, Silent Man,
And he very, very seldom said a word;
He shuddered at the sight
Of the kind of men that write,
For the doer was the chap that he preferred.
When he exercised his troops
He commanded them to run
With abbreviated whoops
Like the popping of a gun,
And they seemed to understand,
Or, at any rate, they ran
Just exactly as he planned,
This extraordinary man,
Though, as far as one could tell,
These electrifying *mots*
Were the simple phrases "Hell!",
"Hell!" and "Ha!" and "Hi!" and
"Ho!",
The ejaculation "Ha!",
The ejaculation "Hi!",
The ejaculation "Hell!",
And. occasionally, "Ho!".

When the Major crossed the wave
He continued to behave
With his customary reticence and strength.
It annoyed him very much
That the Frenchmen and the Dutch
Had a language of unnecessary length.
So in speaking to the Kurds,
Or the Spanish, or the Shah,
He employed the shortest words
Such as "Ho!" and such as "Ha!";
And it answered very well,
For, whichever he had said,
As a rule they rang the bell
And arranged to have him fed.
"Why should any man do more?"
Said the Major. "What's the good,
When a hearty British roar
Can be always understood?
If you bellow at the Shah
The ejaculation 'Ha!',
The interrogation 'Hi?',
Or the observation 'Ho!'?"

But when Reggie fell in love
With a darling, with a dove,
And the moment was approaching to propose,
He was careful to rehearse
An exordium in verse
And a very, very wordy piece of prose.
But his head was in a whirl,
Not a sentence could he say,

So he snorted at the girl
  In his customary way,
Like the starting of a Ford,
  Or the bursting of a cloud,
And I'm sorry to record
  That the lady laughed aloud

She replied, to his surprise,
  Not with "Yes" and not with "No."
But with short explosive cries,
  Very much like "Ha!" and "Ho!",
With the cachinnation "Ha!",
With the mocking sound of "Ho!",
With the cachinnation "Ha!",
  And, occasionally, "Ho!".

Said the lady, "Though I know
The expressions 'Ha!' and 'Ho!'

Are attractive in the ordinary way,
    I imagine that a wife
    Would require in later life
Conversation more elaborate and gay."
    Broken-hearted, he withdrew
      With a bitter little smile,
    With a dictionary too,
      To a distant desert isle,
    Where by practice on the birds
      He is doing what he can
    To acquire the use of words
      Like a literary man,
    Making speeches to the birds
      With a literary flow,
    Though, alas! his favourite words
      Still, I hear, are " Ha !" and " Ho !"–
I am sorry, but it's so,
He is still attached to " Ho !",
The ejaculation " Ha !",
    And the observation " Ho !" .

AFTER-DINNER

I WILL not make a speech to-night,
   I have not had sufficient wine;
It is not just, it is not right
   To ask a fellow out to dine
And treat him in this kind of way—
I *will* not make a speech, I say.

No, Mr. Secretary, *no!*
   Ask Mr. Mudd to say a word,
Let Mr. Mumble have a blow—
   He is not happy, I have heard,
Except when he is on his feet
Extemporising after meat.

But I am very dumb to-night;
   I cannot think of words at all;
My neighbour's eyes are very bright,
   My neighbour's hands are very small,
And, if I did say something, Sir,
I fancy it would be to her.

The wine was good (though, I repeat,
   I have not had enough of it);
I liked the fish, I liked the sweet,
   The company is exquisite;
And that's exactly what I feel
About this admirable meal.

And you are free to write it down
  And put it in the minute-book,
And I will give you half-a-crown
  And you can give it to the cook—
But damned be he who here suggests
That I should answer for The Guests!

My neighbour's eyes are very bright,
  My neighbour's hands are very small,
And I am very gay to-night;
  O Mercy, must we spoil it all?
A speech is long but life is short;
Please go away—and pass the port.

THE POLICEMAN'S SERENADE

A GRAND LITTLE OPERA

Outside a house — Moonlight — Discovered — a
POLICEMAN, *with Lantern, Truncheon and*
Service Guitar.

THE POLICEMAN:

Susan, hear my tuneful sighing,
　　Brightest jewel on my beat,
From your hateful kitchen flying
　　At my bosom find retreat.
See, the moon, serene and argent!
And we need not fear the Sergeant,
　　For he loves a lady too.
Here in pain I stand, my beauty,
One devoted eye on duty,
　　But the other fixed on you.

SUSAN (*emerging*):

Robert, though in my profession
　　We are crude, uncultured, coarse,
In the arts of self-expression
　　Scarcely fit to meet the Force,
In my plain ill-tutored fashion

Let me here declare my passion,
  And if still you doubt my flame,
Robert, see with what sweet ardour,
Leaving chaos in the larder,
  To your dear blue arms I came

THE POLICEMAN:

Now, my girl, I know you're mocking.
  Have you not another swain?
When you hear the postman knocking
  Does your heart not knock again?
When you hear that milkman bellow
Do you still admire the fellow?
  Tell me, love, for, if 'tis so,

Should I meet these men at luncheon
With a buffet from my truncheon
  Robert's rivals go below.

SUSAN:

Robert, cease this foolish clamour:
  Vain the milkman's modish coo!
And in vain do postmen hammer
  If they bring no word from you.
For yourself your Sue is yearning—
But I smell the supper burning,
  Back to duty must I press,
So if you have done with hinting,
You'll oblige me by imprinting
  On my lips a chaste caress.

> [*Chaste caress.* SUSAN *retires into the
>   kitchen.*

THE POLICEMAN:

So, good-night. Sleep sound, my pretty.
  Here till dawn I take my stand;
There are burglars in this city,
  But we have them well in hand;
And whatever fears may furrow
Other foreheads in the borough
  Nothing shall this roof surprise;
Mice and burglars both repelling,
Robert guards the sacred dwelling
  Where his lovely Susan lies.

> [*Exit* THE POLICEMAN, *with lantern, to
>   examine the defences of the house.*
> [*Enter a* MILKMAN, *with Milkcart.*

THE MILKMAN (*softly*):

Milk-O!   Milk-O!
Come, Susan, from thy pots and pans,
   No matter who may chide,
For with his merry tinkling cans
   Thy milkman waits outside,
That brings each morning with his cart
His unadulterated heart
   And softly calls below,
   " Milk-O! my love, Milk-O!"

So fair the night, my love so strong,
   This way I had to walk,
But I have brought my cart along
   That people may not talk;
This pint of milk I'll give to thee
Our little *alibi* to be,
   And softly call below,
   " Milk-O! my love, Milk-O!"

SUSAN (*emerging*):

Is that my milkman?   Did I hear
   That voice so like the linnet's?
O lovely milkman, kiss me, dear
   (I've not been kissed for minutes).

    [THE MILKMAN *gives her a pint of milk
      and a kiss.* THE POLICEMAN, *return-
      ing, observes this transaction with ill-
      concealed concern.*

                       3

THE POLICEMAN (*aside*):

Duped! Duped! Ah, duped! So this is
    Woman's trust.
Revenge, proud Robert! He shall bite the
    dust.

        (*He approaches the guilty pair.*)

Now what's all this here?

THE MILKMAN:

                Officer,
My lawful trade I ply with her.
Of which in witness pray behold
This pint of milk but newly sold.

THE POLICEMAN (*suspiciously*):

In my experience of crime—
And that, my lad, 's a goodish time—
I never saw a stranger sight,
A person selling milk at *night!*
Had it been whisky, now, or silk,
I might have winked at it—but MILK!

SUSAN:

Unhand him, wretch!

THE POLICEMAN:

            My girl, withdraw!
It's my belief he's broke the law;
Men don't sell pints of milk by chance—
It's a suspicious circumstance.
And what is more, you amorous gurgler,
You'll be arrested for a burglar.

But first, that nothing be mistook,
I'll note the details in my book.

> [*He does so.   Meanwhile* THE MILKMAN
> *sings a passionate farewell.*

THE MILKMAN:

Farewell, my heart, farewell;
  To Pentonville I go,
But in my gloomy cell
  One comfort I may know—
Outside the dungeon dark,
If you will sit and hark,
I'll now and then remark
  " Milk-O ! my love, Milk-O !"

SUSAN:

Outside the dungeon dark
I'll sit at eve and hark,
And hope that you'll remark
  " Milk-O ! my love, Milk-O !"

THE POLICEMAN (*taking notes*):

Though he is in the dark
This ill-conditioned spark
Will now and then remark
  " Milk-O ! my love, Milk-O !"

> [*During this affecting scene a* BURGLAR,
> *seizing his opportunity, enters the house
> by the open kitchen door.*
> [*Emotional   music.*   THE   POLICEMAN
> *marches* THE MILKMAN *off with cart.*

SUSAN (*reflective*):

Alas, in one short night
    To lose two lovers true!
O Cupid, is this right?
    I put the point to you.
My Milkman in a cage—
My Robert in a rage,
O Cupid, at this stage
    What is a girl to do?

[THE BURGLAR *emerges from the house
carrying a Bag containing Swag.*

THE BURGLAR (*presenting pistol*):

Be silent, hussy, for if you should shout
The chances are you'll have your brains blown
    out.

SUSAN (*unmoved—curiously*):

The voice is sweet,
Well-formed the feet
The figure has a grace,
One boon I ask—
Remove your mask,
That I may see the face.

(*Reassuring*):

To jail I will not shove you,
For I believe I love you.

[THE BURGLAR, *struck by her beauty and
courage, removes his mask, while his
revolver falls from his nerveless fingers.*

THE BURGLAR:

Now strike me pink in every limb and feature
If e'er I saw a more attractive creature!

SUSAN (*after examining the face, picks up
the revolver*):

Yes, I love you, burglar dear,
    Burglar, will you marry me?

You have money, it is clear,
    I have brains for two or three.
Burglar, if you will not wed,
I shall shoot you through the head!
Better marr-i-ed than dead—
    Pretty burglar, marry me!

THE BURGLAR:

Never in my varied life
    Saw I such a tiger-cat:

Born to be a burglar's wife—
   And I can't say more than that.
You can drop the pistol now
(It's not loaded, anyhow).
I'll propose, if you'll allow.
   Pretty housemaid, marry me!

BOTH:

To the booty of the day
   Let me add one precious kiss,
With our treasure then away—
   But no burgling after this!
Burgling is, in fact, a bore;
Safe upon some foreign shore
We'll be happy evermore—

   Pretty {burglar, housemaid,} marry me!

> [*They go off, rapturous, with Bag of Swag.*
> [THE POLICEMAN *returns, philosophical, having jugged* THE MILKMAN, *and resumes his vigil.*

THE POLICEMAN:

Frail, ah, frail! But I forgive her.
   Here till dawn I play my part.
So no other evil-liver
   Shall attempt her guileless heart,
And whatever fears may furrow
Other foreheads in the borough

Nothing shall this roof surprise,
Mice and burglars both repelling,
Through the night I'll guard the dwelling
  Where my lovely Susan lies.

CURTAIN.

" VINOVI "

A Song for the Vendor of a Patent Medicine

Sir or Madam, are you well?
Yes, we know it's hard to tell;
Like as not you fondly think,
Madam, you are in the pink,
But, conceal it how we please,
Most of us have *some* disease.
Frankly, Sir, the chances are
You have cancer or catarrh;
Madam, in our humble view,
There is something wrong with *you*.
Never mind—we'd like to bet
" Vinovi " will save you yet.

For nervousness, lassitude, debility, anæmia,
Quinsy, sciatica, discomfort when you dine,
Rheumatism, dandruff, acute septicæmia,
The measles, the mumps,
The dropsy and the dumps,
Melancholy, flatulence, a tendency to pine.
Take a little " Vinovi,"
Take a little " Vinovi,"
And take it in a glass of wine.

Madam, Sir, it's safe to say
You have one of these to-day.

Sir, be not afraid of us,
Madam, we need not discuss
Which exactly you have got—
" Vinovi " will cure the lot.
Do you suffer much from fits,
Meningitis, nerves or nits?
Does your work repel you?   Quite.
" Vinovi " will put you right.
Are you skinny, Sir, or fat?
" Vinovi " will stop all that.

For nervousness, lassitude and glandular scirrhosity,
Quinsy, sciatica, discomfort when you dine,
Rheumatism, baldness, congenital verbosity,
The colic and the croup,
The shingles and the stoop,
Melancholy, flatulence, a tendency to pine,
Take a little " Vinovi,"
Take a little " Vinovi,"
And take it in a glass of wine.

Sir or Madam, have a care!
There are tricksters everywhere.
Sir or Madam, do not take
" Equibos," for pity's sake!
Neither, though you've bought a tin,
Drink a drop of " Vigorin "!
This is made of mice, of *course;*
" Equibos " is simply horse.
So is " Nervinu "; and then
" Nervinu " is one-and-ten.
" Vinovi " is one-and-nine,
And you take the stuff with wine.

3 *

For nervousness, lassitude, debility, anæmia;
  Quinsy, sciatica, discomfort when you dine,
Rheumatism, rickets and chronic septicæmia,
    For tetanus and thrush,
    Garrulity and gush,
  Free Trade, flatulence, obesity, decline,
    Take a little " Vinovi,"
    Take a little " Vinovi,"
  And take it in a glass of wine.

Madam, Sir, you may be sure
"Vinovi" is good and pure;
Madam, we do not include
Harmful gases in this food;
"Vinovi" does *not* contain
Boric acid, bats or bane,
Nor, as many people think,
Is it made of marking-ink,
But from herbs and bits of hay—
How or why I must not say.
Anyhow, it's pure because
Dr. Dumble said it was.

For nervousness, lassitude, paralysis, precocity,
  Quinsy, sciatica, discomfort when you dine,
Toothache, aphasia, congenital verbosity,
    The measles, the mumps,
    The jaundice and the jumps,
  Insanity and flatulence, senility, decline,
    Take a little " Vinovi,"
    Take a little " Vinovi,"
  And take it in a glass of wine.

Not with shudders, not with squeals,
Not with water after meals—
Take it gaily while you dine,
Wash it down with draughts of wine.
Otherwise it will not act—
That is odd, but that's a fact.
Take a tablet in some port,
Your diseases will be short;
Take a couple in champagne,
You will not be ill again.
(" Vinovi," we need not say,
Must be taken thrice a day.)

For nervousness, lassitude, debility, anæmia,
  Quinsy, sciatica, insomnia and strain,
Rheumatism, baldness, acute septicæmia,
      For tetanus and thrush,
      Garrulity and gush,
  Melancholy, flatulence and water on the brain,
        Take a little " Vinovi,"
        Take a little " Vinovi,"
      And take it in the best champagne.

THE PROUD HUSBAND

My love, I am so proud of you,
I want the world to love you too.
My heart cries out to every man,
" This is my own, my lovely Ann!
And you are blind that pass her by
If you be not bewitched as I.
Look, look again—her eyes so rare,
Her face, her feet—confess her fair!"
I want the world to love you too,
But am tormented if they do.

So happy I in loving you,
I would the world were happy too.
My heart goes out to any man
That vainly loves my lovely Ann;
And you may smile and smile again
If this will ease the victim's pain.
But if that smile too soft appear,
I'll strike the victim dead, my dear.
I want the world to love you too,
But Heaven help the men who do!

SAVE THE TIGER!

WHEN Lady Jane refused to be
The wife of Viscount Fiddledee
He rose abruptly from his knee
   And said, " Excuse this bungle—
I think I will not stay to dine,
There is a train at half-past nine;
To-morrow by the fastest line
   I'm leaving for the jungle.

     " Ho, varlet, run and pack my gun,
      My passport pray discover;
     I mean to shoot some savage brute
      To show how much I love her.
     Far off in India's poisoned swamps
     Some unsuspecting tiger romps,
      Condemned to die;
      And you know why—
     'Cos you won't marry me.
     Oh, ain't you got no heart, my gal?
     Think of that dumb animal.
      Save that tiger,
      Poor dumb tiger,
     Save that tiger—marry me!

" I'll hunt him down on shiny nights
With cunning telescopic sights,

And, if the creature turns and bites,
　As is his cruel fashion,
I'll lie content and let him chew,
A-thinking all the time of you;
For what's the worst that he can do
　Compared with hopeless passion?

> *" Ho, varlet, run and pack my gun,*
> 　*My lovely one rejects me.*
> *I kind of ache to shoot a snake,*
> 　*For that's how it affects me.*
> *With battle-axe and blunderbuss*
> *I'll hip the hippopotamus;*
> 　*Some buffalo*
> 　*Has got to go*
> 　*Because you won't be mine.*
> *Heartless one, I'm better dead,*
> *But think of them dumb quadruped;*
> 　*Save that python,*
> 　*Save that hippo,*
> 　*Save that buffalo—be mine!"*

The Lady Jane began to cry;
The thought of hippopotami
Unnaturally doomed to die
　Had stirred her woman's pity.
She married him.　And till this day,
Whenever he would have his way,
He only has to sing or say
　This moving little ditty:

> *" Ho, pack my gun, you naughty one!*
> 　*Although I love you madly,*

SAVE THE TIGER!

I'm off to shoot some savage brute,
*   You do behave so badly.*
I'd like to beat you, but you'd laugh,
I'll take it out of some giraffe,
*   Some buffalo*
*   Has got to go*
*   Because you won't be good.*
Ain't you got no heart, dear wife?
You can't approve of taking life—
*   Then save that tiger,*
*   Poor dumb tiger,*
*   Save that buffalo—be good!"*

THE PERSON-IN-THE-MOON

WHENE'ER I see your face,
            Mr. Moon,
So like a large grimace,
            Mr. Moon,
So like the man next-door,
I wonder more and more
What everything is for,
            Mr. Moon.

Proud is your yellow eye,
            Mr. Moon,
But I cannot think why,
            Mr. Moon,
For it is sad but true
We don't think much of you;
Such awful things you do,
            Mr. Moon!

Taught by that artful ray,
            Mr. Moon,
What silly things we say,
            Mr. Moon!
How many a fatal Miss
We simply have to kiss!
Oh, are you proud of this,
            Mr. Moon?

When men go wild or worse,
      Mr. Moon,
When widows take to verse,
      Mr. Moon,
When couples sit and coo
In several feet of dew,
We put it down to you,
      Mr. Moon.

And I for one don't know,
      Mr. Moon,
Why poets praise you so,
      Mr. Moon;
Strong is your sway and wide,
Love—lunatics—the tide—
But *are* they food for pride,
      Mr. Moon?

How are we to tell,
      Mr. Moon,
You're not to blame as well,
      Mr. Moon,
For income-tax and gin,
The tumbril and the twin,
And cinemas and sin,
      Mr. Moon?

What are you, after all,
      Mr. Moon?
A large malignant ball,
      Mr. Moon;

Can you recall a case
Where such a smiling face
Concealed a soul so base,
   Mr. Moon?

That face I cannot read,
   Mr. Moon;
Are you a man indeed,
   Mr. Moon?
Is there or is there not
A woman on the spot?
This would explain a lot,
   Mr. Moon.

SAUSAGE AND MASH

IF there's a dish
For which I wish
More frequent than the rest,
If there's a food
On which I brood
When starving or depressed,
If there's a thing that life can give
Which makes it worth our while to live,
If there's an end
On which I'd spend
My last remaining cash,
It's sausage, friend,
It's sausage, friend,
It's sausage, friend, and mash.

Sausage and mash,
Sausage and mash,
Hope of the hungry and joy of the just!
Sausage and mash,
(Not haddock or hash),
Done till they bubble and done till they
bust!
Your truffles are toys,
Your oysters are trash
Contrasted, my boys,
With the homelier joys,

64

The beauty, the poise,
Of sausage and mash.

O noble thing,
From churl to king,
Uniting class and clan!
What brow so high
We cannot spy
The simple sausage-fan?
The haughty plumber blows a kiss
When Mrs. Plumber brings him this;
And where's the Lord
So old and bored
But that proud eye will flash
If some sweet girl
Says, " Sausage, Earl?
A sausage, Earl, and mash?"

Sausage and mash,
Sausage and mash,
With an R in the month I am happy and
gay!
Sausage and mash,
My molars I gnash
With impotent longing in August and
May!
I weary of fish,
I deprecate hash,
Your partridges—pish!
Quite frankly I wish
For the tiniest dish
Of sausage and mash.

Sweet when we rise
With heavy eyes
And work is just ahead;
Sweet any time,
But most sublime
When we should be in bed;
Though kingdoms rise and kingdoms set
A sausage is a sausage yet;
When Love is dead,
Ambition fled,
And Pleasure, lad, and Pass.,
You'll still enjoy
A sausage, boy,
A sausage, boy, and mash.

Sausage and mash,
Sausage and mash,
Done till they bubble and done till they
bust!
Sausage and mash,
Careless and rash,
I raises my hat to the food of the just!
What's women to me,
What's liquor or cash?
Contented are we,
The sons of the free,
With a pot of hot tea
And sausage and mash!

THE DUBIOUS BACHELOR

A Rather Sad Statistical Song

I WILL not live another year
  A sad and solitary he!
I long to call some damsel dear,
  But, goodness, which is it to be?
Such charmers everywhere I find,
Delicious, beautiful and kind,
But I can NOT make up my mind—

> *For there are eighteen million women
> in England and Wales, and one of
> these is, presumably, my soul-mate.*

But I am dismal after dark;
  It *is* a dismal thing to sit
And think of many a good remark
  With no one there to laugh at it:
The flat is full of ticking clocks,
The very mouse comes out and mocks,
And no one seems to mend my socks,

> *Though there are eighteen million
> women in England and Wales, and
> one of these is, presumably, my soul-
> mate.*

Then I will take my Phyllis out,
    And we will dance till three or four,
For Phyllis likes me, not a doubt,
    And I like Phyllis more and more,

For she is sweet and she is gay,
Though she has nothing much to say,
And she would suit me, in a way,

> *But there are eighteen million women in
> England and Wales, and one of these
> is, presumably, my soul-mate.*

And when I gaze in Mary's eyes
    Poor Phyllis seems a little thing,

For Mary is so very wise
  And she can play and she can sing;
But, dear, oh dear, she cannot smile,
And she is not at all my style,
And I am thinking all the while

    That there are eighteen million women
      in England and Wales, and one of
      these is, presumably, my soul-mate.

Then there is Miss Camelia Mole,
  And I have asked her once or twice,
But she is like the Arctic Pole,
  Though she is uniformly nice,
And she is fond, and so am I,
But if I ask until I die
I know that she will still reply

    That there are seventeen million men in
      England and Wales, and one of these
      is, presumably, her soul-mate.

Ah me!   But come, I'll not despair;
  By April—well, at least by May,
I'll marry *somebody*, I swear,
  And we'll be happy, I dare say;
For Phyllis is a little pet,
And Mary *may* amuse me yet,
And I'll endeavour to forget

    That there are eighteen million women
      in England and Wales, and one of
      these is, presumably, my soul-mate.

Yet oft, how often, in the street,
　　Or riding on the District line,
I see a maid so rare and sweet
　　I *know* that she was meant for mine.
She knows it not.   She leaves the train,
I never see her face again.
Why should I ?   Well, I don't complain—

　　　　But there are eighteen million women in
　　　　　　England and Wales, and one of these
　　　　　　is, presumably, my soul-mate.

Ah, Phyllis, when you name the day,
　　Or Mary dear (whiche'er it be),
To some lone island let's away
　　Where there is not another she ;
That I may never, never view
A girl more glorious than you,
For I will promise to be true—

　　　　But all the same there are eighteen mil-
　　　　　　lion women in England and Wales,
　　　　　　and one of these is, presumably, my
　　　　　　soul-mate.

THE ENGLISHMAN

A VERY PATRIOTIC SONG

AIR: *"Here's a health unto His Majesty."*

WHEN Earth in Eden did awake
  And Man was made and mated,
The earliest men, by some mistake,
  Were foreigners all created;
And in this fix the world began,
Till Heaven conceived a nobler plan
And there was born an Englishman—

> *With a fa, la, la, fa, la, la, la, la, la, la,*
> *With a fa, la, la, la, la, la, la!*

Still half the sphere in darkness sat,
  But Britons went and found it;
The heathen swore the Earth was flat—
  We flung the flag all round it;
And if the sea, with stealthy care,
Threw up an island anywhere,
An Englishman was always there—

> *With a fa, la, la, fa, la, la, la, la, la, la,*
> *With a fa, la, la, la, la, la, la!*

Then round the globe we looked, and lo!
  The foreigners did not shave, Sir,
Nor did we shrink from saying so
  In accents bold and brave, Sir;
We pointed out from day to day
What we should do if we were they—
We made them love us in this way—

    With a fa, la, la, fa, la, la, la, la, la, la,
    With a fa, la, la, la, la, la, la!

And I am tempted, I confess,
  To self-congratulation
When I reflect that I possess
  The virtues of my nation,
And daily let my neighbours see
How different their lives might be
If they would but be ruled by me—

    With a fa, la, la, fa, la, la, la, la, la, la,
    With a fa, la, la, la, la, la, la!

The simple mind and manly air,
  Not Brains so much as Breeding,
With *joie de vivre* and *savoir faire,*
  Are constantly succeeding;
Not men of words, we live to do,
Nor speak till we are spoken to,
Then answer "Cock-a-doodle-doo!"—

    With a fa, la, la, fa, la, la, la, la, la, la,
    With a fa, la, la, la, la, la, la!

Alas, for all our kindly pain,
    The world is sick and sore, Sir,
And Frenchmen mulishly remain
    As foreign as before, Sir.
Thus ends the tale as it began;
Conceive the difference, if you can,
Had Adam been an Englishman—

> *With a fa, la, la, fa, la, la, la, la, la, la,*
> *With a fa, la, la, la, la, la, la!*

GOING TO THE DOGS

YOU don't know what a woman's love can do,
                        Joanna,
   To keep a chap from his decline and fall;
I've been a better man since I met you,
                        Joanna,
   And I don't think I've hardly sinned at all;
      If I'm to stay like this for life,
                        Joanna,
         It means you gotter be my little wife—

            For if you won't be mine,
            Then I shall take to wine,
I'll be a bad man, because I love you so;
   I'll drink yellow drinks in low-down places,
   I'll take no exercise and go to the races,
   I'll go to Africa, I'll shoot a tiger,
   I'll eat drugs on the banks of the Niger,
   I'll make faces and I'll make scenes,
   I'll put counters in the slot-machines,
   I'll waste my substance and borrow from the Jews,
   I'll dress slovenly and wear brown shoes,
   I won't worry how I look—d'you see?
   I'll let my hair grow and shave after tea.

To the dogs,
To the dogs,
To the bad black dogs,
To the bad black abominable dogs I'll go,
And all for the love of my sweet Jo!

What—you won't be mine?
Then I shall go and dine.
I'll be a bad man, because I love you so.
  I'll take pretty girls away from their mothers,
  I'll buy a Wireless and interfere with others,
  I'll drink Crême de Menthe in great big beakers,
  I'll go to meetings and interrupt the speakers,
  I won't shrink from gross exaggeration;
  And I won't make no polite conversation;
  I'll be a bounder, a Bohemian, a boob,
  And I *won't* stand up for women in the Tube;

I'll lie abed late, meditating crimes,
I'll vote Liberal and write to *The Times.*

> *To the dogs,*
> *To the dogs,*
> *To the bad black dogs,*
> *To the bad black abominable dogs I'll go,*
> *And all for the love of my sweet Jo!*

What—you *will* be mine?
Then you shall see me shine.
I'll be a good boy, because I love you so.
I'll wear white spats and I'll play cricket,
I'll travel third with a first-class ticket,
I'll give money to the starving Prussians,
I'll make a gesture and pray for the Russians;
I'll be a high-brow, but I'll look hearty,
And I won't laugh at the Liberal Party;
I'll wake up with a carol in my throat,
And I'll go to bed on a high top-note;
I'll take a tumbler of water in the morning,
I'll help cook when the cook gives warning,
I'll be a little ray of sunshine, dear,
And I'll make money, shall we say, next year?
I won't kiss nobody without your permission,
I'll go twice to the Wembley Exhibition,
I'll eat apples as I ought to do,
I'll drink lemonade and I'll love you.

> *To the dogs,*
> *To the dogs,*
> *To the good grey dogs,*
> *To the good grey gentlemanly dogs I'll go,*
> *And all for the love of my sweet Jo!*

THE PITEOUS BALLAD OF ARABELLA BOOLEY

OH, have you heard my horrid tale? Young women
 all, attend.
Will Wilkinsop he courted me for seven years on end,
Then up says he, "Enough of that," and to the
 church went we—
Alas, we wed at half-past four instead of ten to three,
 Ah, we was wed at half-past four instead of ten to
 three.

The bride was fair, the guests was there, but Parson
 he was dead
From riding on a wicked horse and falling on his
 head;
Two-forty-one the deed was done, and by the law,
 d'ye see?
No English man with English maid may marry after
 three,
 No English lad on English soil shall marry after
 three.

Then "Up, my lads," my father cries, "though we
 must mourn his case,
Go forth and find some clergy kind to take the poor
 man's place!

My daughter Nan has caught a man and married she
    shall be.
Go, brother Jock, and stop the clock ten minutes short
    of three."
    And Uncle Jock he stopped the clock ten minutes
    short of three.

The sun was low, the moon also, which greatly did
    annoy,
When back comes Thomas Wilkinsop with a bit of a
    clergy-boy;
" It's growing dark," he made remark.   " It's early
    yet," said we,
For by the light of the moon (though slight) the clock
    said ten to three:
    By the light of the moon that afternoon the time
    was ten to three.

The clergy-boy he wished us joy and straight he mar-
    ried we;
We vowed our vows and rode away to Bungay by
    the sea,
And William there he swore a swear—" True man
    and wife we be,
Though we was wed, as I've heard said, considerable
    after three;
    You be my bride, though we was tied considerable
    after three."

Two days go by, and there was I a-pleading for a kiss,
When in there walks the Bishop of my William's
    diocese.

"Good morning," said his Reverence; "no man and
  wife you be,
For you was wed, as I've heard said, considerable
  after three,
  *Oh, you was wed," the Bishop said, " considerable
  after three.*

"It don't apply," continued he, to put us at our ease,
" To christenings and funerals and functions such as
  these.
I'd bury you at ten or two, and buried you would be,
But weddings must be finished just before the hour of
  three,
  *Ah, weddings, unlike funerals, must not be after
  three."*

"Is that a fact?" said Wilkinsop.—"The facts are
  as I state;
I much regret you're single yet, but still it's not too
  late.
Pray finish, Miss, that lawless kiss, and travel home
  with me,
And you shall vow your vows again at twenty-five to
  three."
  *Oh, you must vow your vows again at twenty-five
  to three."*

"One moment, pray," said William then, to my
  extreme dismay,
" This child of Eve, I now perceive, though pleasing
  for a day,

Is not the wife I'd have for life, and, if as how I'm
free,

I must decline to make her mine at twenty-five to
three,

*Oh, I decline to make her mine at twenty-five to
three.*"

The Bishop took his bell and book, and cursed him
up and down;

With sobs and tears I pulled his ears, and then he left
the town.

And all he said was, "I was wed; if wed no more
I be,

'Twere mad, it's plain, to wed again at twenty-five
to three,

I don't intend to wed again at twenty-five to three."

Oh, cursed are the cruel laws!   O deary, deary me!

Oh, what a life!   Not maid nor wife, nor widow, yet
all three!

My daughter begs from door to door, a child of shame
is she,

For I was wed at half-past four instead of ten to three,

*Oh, I was wed at half-past four instead of ten to
three!*

DON'T TELL MY MOTHER I'M LIVING IN SIN; OR, SEE WHAT IT DONE TO ME!

A SONG FOR THE SOCIETY FOR THE SUPPRESSION OF WICKEDNESS AND DANCING

Beside a empty barrel
  Upon a foreign shore
There sat the wreck of a 'uman man,
  A 'uman man no more;
An opium pipe was in his hand,
  He had not shaved for days,
The pack of cards that strewed the sand
  The horrid truth displays,
When " Why," says I, " if that ain't Ned!"
He raised his bloodshot eyes and said:

" Don't tell my mother I'm living in sin,
  Don't let the old folks know:
Don't tell my twin that I breakfast on gin,
  He'd never survive the blow.
Promise you'll keep little Maggie from harm;
You'll have to take care with a girl of her charm;
Don't let her know about whisky and ' snow,'
DON'T let her go to them clubs in Soho!
But tell the whole world of the ruin you see;
This is what comes of a night at the Embassy—
  See what it done for me!"

82

The broken reed continued :
    " I never swore a swore,
I never kissed a woman's hand
    Till I was twenty-four.
They took me to a night-club then—
    Ah, how was a lad to know ?—
And all the rips of Wimbledon
    Was dancing in a row;
A so-called haunt of pleasure—see ?
And it was that what done for me."

      " Don't tell my mother," etc.

" Nine—ten—eleven-thirty—
    And still the music played.
O Heavens, the mushroom-sandwiches,
    The lights, the lemonade !
And a chit of an actress-girl was there—
    I was only a moon-struck calf;
Next day I stop at a postcard-shop
    And I bought her photograph !
The shame of it !" the sinner sighed.
" Cheer up !" says I, but he replied—

      " Don't tell my mother," etc.

" Once only," said the drunkard,
    " But once was all too oft;
Temptation's cruel, cruel hard,
    Particler if you're soft.
Drink, women, drugs, revolvers, knives—
    I took the downward track,
So here I am with seven wives,
    And most of them are black."

" Ah, don't say that," said I to Ned.
" I do say that," said he, he said—

" *But don't tell my mother I'm living in sin,*
    Don't let the old folks know:
Don't tell my twin that I breakfast on gin,
    He'd never survive the blow.
Promise you'll keep little Maggie from harm;
You'll have to take care with a girl of her charm;
Don't let her know about whisky and ' snow,'
DON'T *let her go to them clubs in Soho!*
But tell the whole world of the ruin you see;
This is what comes of a night at the Embassy—
    See what it done for me!"

WEAR YOUR WHITE

Wear your white, my love, to-night,
  Wear that little frock you wore
When I met you, long ago.
Satin—silk? I hardly know,
  But I saw you at the door
        And I loved you—
      Still I love you,
Wear your white, my love, to-night,

Wear your white, my love, to-night,
  You were young and lovely then,
  Bright your eye and sweet your smile,
And I wondered all the while
    Did you like those other men?
        For I loved you—
      Still I love you,
Wear your white, my love, to-night,

Wear your white, my love, to-night,
  Out of fashion? I'll not know.
Old and faded? I'll not see.
It's the fashion still for me,
  Thus I met you, long ago,
      And I loved you—
      Still I love you,
Wear your white, my love, to-night,

RING IN THE OLD!

LINES FOR A DISAPPOINTED MAN AT A FANCY DRESS REVEL ON NEW YEAR'S EVE

COME, let every jolly fellow,
  Whatsoever his disguise,
    All the Courtiers, Clowns, Divines,
    All the Queens and Columbines,
  Let them sing and bawl and bellow
    While this Old Deceiver dies.

Here, festooned with coloured paper,
  Here, deserted by my dear,
    Here, beside the rifled bar,
    In the costume of a tar,
  While the young things coo and caper,
    Here will I revile the year.

Kindly clock, fly fast and faster!
  Horrid, hateful '23,
    Other persons may or may
    Not have flourished in your day,
  I can think of no disaster
    Which has not occurred to me.

87

Crossed in love in January;
  February—deep in debt;
    March—I fell in love with Jane;
    April—over-drawn again;
May—I fell in love with Mary,
  And the year's not over yet.

Summer saw me sad and thinner;
  Jane was married in July;
    June—I bought a share—it fell,
    Till the day I chose to sell,
August—I'd have backed a winner,
  But I knew the horse would die.

There have been depressing pages
  In my history before;
    Other winters acted base,
    But I don't recall a case
When I seemed to work such ages
  And was so extremely poor.

'23, to think what revels
  Twelve months back saluted thee!
    I was then a Persian Prince;
    Joan has never loved me since.
All the most unpleasant devils
  Fly away with '23!

So farewell. Few hopes I cherish,
  Yet shall Britons ne'er complain.
    '23, a glass of wine!
    Here's a pretty Columbine—
Ten to one, before you perish,
  I shall be in love again.

MR. TURPENTINE

BRING me an oyster, bring me five or six,
　Bring me a bottle of the best white wine,
Bring me a sole done up with fancy-tricks—
　Let me, in short, most generously dine;
　　And then, when I am warm and fed,
　　When all the world looks round and red,
　　Fill up, and solemnly be said
　A hideous curse on Mr. Turpentine!

Confound you, Mr. Turpentine!
Confound you, Mr. Turpentine!
Confound you, Mr. Turpentine,
*　Misfortune dog your name!*
*　　Rats bite your nails,*
*　　And hairy scales*
*　Appear upon your frame!*
May any horse which you select
Have some congenital defect,
*　　And at the post*
*　　Give up the ghost*
*　Or suddenly be lame!*
*　　May Bulls and Bears*
*　　Mess up your shares,*
And, if some foolish girl

Has sweetly smiled upon you, oh!
May she incontinently throw
You over for an Earl!
O may your nose go red and shine!
O may you catch a chill!
Confound you, Mr. Turpentine!
I wish you very ill!

No, do not ask the details of his case
  Nor what gross injury the man has done;
It were a shame to tell you in this place;
  I simply mention that he fouls the sun.
    Then drink your healths, fill, drink the
      King,
    Drink Church and State, drink anything,
    But fill again, and madly sing
An awful doom for Mr. Turpentine!

Confound you, Mr. Turpentine!
Confound you, Mr. Turpentine!
Confound you, Mr. Turpentine,
The Furies do you brown!
O may you buy
When things are high,
And sell when they are down!
O may the Inland Revenue
Conceive a strong dislike for you,
And sometimes hale
You off to jail
For owing half-a-crown!
And when you pass
A looking-glass
O may you start and cry

With new conviction every night,
"That is a most unpleasant sight—
My goodness, is it I?"
O may your nose go red and shine!
O may you catch a chill!
Confound you, Mr. Turpentine,
I wish you very ill!

Alas, a mellowness pervades my brain;
How fatal is the influence of wine!
My darned good-nature moves in me again,
I cannot curse you, Mr. Turpentine!
Nay, Turpentine, I sigh for you.
Though I detest the things you do,
You cannot help yourself, it's true—
Ah, let us pray for Mr. Turpentine!

O bless you, Mr. Turpentine!
O bless you, Mr. Turpentine!
O bless you, Mr. Turpentine,
I wish you well and fair!
Good angels take
Your face and make
Some suitable repair;
Good fairies wrestle with your mind
And leave you sweet and clean and kind,
But may you not
Discover what
A horrid thing you were!
May men applaud
Your vilest fraud
And trust you once again;

And may that fond and foolish girl
Abandon her beloved Earl
And live with you in Spain!
O Turpentine, a glass of wine!
What use is it to curse?
God made you, Mr. Turpentine,
And how can man do worse?

A RESOLUTION

I SHOULD have been a business man.
The will to win, the power to plan,
    The cool commanding touch,
The bold design, the ruthless tongue—
All these were mine when I was young,
    And people said as much;
But there, I have a gentle heart,
And then I have some truck with Art,
    So fatal to Success;
And I will not conceal from you
That from a business point of view
    I flourish less and less.
But let me add, most loud and clear,
I WILL be businesslike this year.

Oh, I will punctually pay
    All taxes, rates and bills,
And answer letters every day
    And light my pipe with spills,
And I will be most circumspect
    In every little thing,
And conscientiously collect
Brown-paper, pins and string,
And do each morning, when I rise,
Some scientific exercise,
    And ten times touch my toes,

95

A RESOLUTION

And every evening will commit
To memory some useful bit
    Of poetry (or prose),
Give up the gambling, drink and dope,
    Pursue the frugal path,
And never, never leave the soap
    Dissolving in the bath.

And, when a fellow tells me flat
    The several reasons why,
What with the price of this and that,
    He cannot sell (or buy)
On any terms that *I* propose,
Or, pop! his tiny profit goes,
And he has creditors in rows,
And like as not the works will close,
    His wife decline and die
(With many miscellaneous woes
    I need not specify)—
Oh, then I will not blow my nose,
    I will not sit and cry,

I will not act like other worms—
I say, I WILL NOT HAVE his terms,
    But with a steely eye
I will confront him, stern and proud,
And I will answer, very loud,
"Hell! cut it out! You lie!"

These are, I know, the methods which
Make other men extremely rich;
And thus do I resolve to steer
My steady course throughout the year.

THE LADIES' BAR

"AS I WAS SAYING ONLY YESTERDAY . . ."

So pore old Mr. Grummet's passed away,
         Mrs. Thomas,
And all from eating unripe plums, they say,
         Mrs. Thomas;
         It's funny, don't you think,
         He never touched the drink,
         And yet he had to die,
         As it might be you or I,
         Mrs. Thomas.

As I was saying only yesterday,
         Mrs. Thomas,
  It isn't any use to fight our fates.
         Well, if it isn't gin
         Was meant to do us in,
  The chances are it's lemonade or dates.
You never saw such saints as my two brothers,
  Yet both of them are dead and gone, my
    dear;
Teetot'lers seem to die the same as others,
  So what's the use of knocking off the
    beer?

To think that Mr. Grummet's on the shelf,
   Mrs. Thomas!
And him so very careful of himself,
   Mrs. Thomas.
  Bed early all his life,
  And never struck his wife,
  It's sad he's dead and done—
  Let's have another one,
   Mrs. Thomas.

As I was saying only yesterday,
   Mrs. Thomas,
 It isn't only drink that does the harm,
   There's Mrs. Pilchard took
   To praying for her cook,
 And after that she fell and broke her arm!
I never see such saints as my two brothers,
 But both of them had asthma bad, my dear;
Teetot'lers seem to suffer, same as others,
 So what's the use of knocking off the beer?

It only shows how careful one should be,
   Mrs. Thomas;
It's flying in the face of Nature, see,
   Mrs. Thomas?
  If he'd been sitting here
  With half a pint of beer,
  Would he have ate that plum
  And gone to Kingdom Come,
   Mrs. Thomas?

As I was saying only yesterday,
   Mrs. Thomas,

Suppose we didn't take our little drops?
All very well for us,
But can't you hear the fuss?
Well, what about the men that grow the hops?
Well, what I mean, we've got to think of others,
It isn't only you and me, my dear.
No doubt the brewers has to keep their mothers,
So where's the sense in knocking off the beer?

"HE DIDN'T OUGHTER . . ."

I NEVER will complain of my dear husband, Mrs.
Henn;
When Wilkinson is sober he's no worse than other
men;
We've never had no serious unpleasantness, but
there—
It's little things, I've always said, are cruellest to
bear.

> *Well, he didn't oughter strike me, not at meals;*
> *I told him of it only yesterday;*
> *It's little things like that a woman feels;*
> *Why can't he wait till dinner's cleared away?*

Of course he takes a drop too much, I don't complain
of that,
It's what I call the bagatelles that knocks a woman
flat;
I don't begrudge the man his beer, though now and
then he's blind,
But he doesn't seem to understand the workings of my
mind.

> *Well, he didn't oughter come to bed in boots—*
> *It's little things that fidget me, you see;*
> *I never mind his sleeping in his suits,*
> *But why can't he sleep in stockings, same*
> *as me?*

The first two months, I *will* say, he was everything
    that's good;
He's carried on with one or two—well, anybody
    would;
The lodger's wife's the latest, and I daresay she's to
    blame—
Well, let him have his fun, I says, but can't he play
    the game?

And he didn't oughter kiss her when I'm there;
A woman has her pride when all is said;
It's little things are cruellest to bear—
Why can't he wait till I've gone up to bed?

TWO DRINKING SONGS

I.—OLD STYLE (THE HEARTY AND UNASHAMED)

DEFEND me from the monkish state!
   Who cannot virtuous be,
But safe behind a cloister's gate,
   What kind of saint is he?
God made a man to roam the earth
   And Eve to be his wife,
And gave him sins to try his worth,
   And love to rule his life.

Does Heav'n send sages by design
   And jesters by mischance?
Why grow our feet so frisky fine
   If we were not to dance?
God made a girl to kiss and cling
   And fill the world with strife,
He gave us all a voice to sing
   And love to rule our life.

Then I will drink to your good health
   And you shall drink to mine;
God never made the grape by stealth,
   We'll not conceal the wine.

He never made a laughing man
  And meant that man to croak;
Then I shall chuckle while I can,
  And you shall be the joke.

II.—NEW STYLE

COME, let us fill the flowing bowl
  And let who can be jolly,
Though poets think it fine to drink,
  We know that it is folly.
Their Bacchus let them call divine,
  But we'll with reason revel,

Confessing while we swill the wine
  That Bacchus is the devil.

> *Fill the cup—there's no excuse,*
> *For wine's the devil, wine's the deuce!*
> *Fill, but let me give you warning,*
> *You'll be sorry in the morning.*
> *Wine's a poison, wine's a bane;*
> *Here's good health—and fill again!*

'Tis Bacchus wrecks the poor man's life
  With base unwholesome cravings,
By Bacchus led he stabs his wife
  And spends the woman's savings.
His children's bread he sells for ale,
  Then, flushed with this enjoyment,
He cuts his throat and goes to jail,
  Thus losing his employment.

> *Then fill the cup, etc.*

The rich as well, 'tis shame to tell,
  When Bacchus blows up breezy,
Play cards and curse and, what is worse,
  Make love a lot too easy;
So many a Viscount seeks his cot
  Unconscious in his carriage,
Without his hat and, like as not,
  Entangled in a marriage.

> *Then fill the cup, etc.*

In fact, with rich and poor the same,
    When horrid fates attack us,
Whatever else may be to blame
    The chances are it's Bacchus;

He rots the liver, saps the soul,
    Makes fortunes run like rivers;
But come, let's fill the flowing bowl,
    For life is more than livers!

    Then fill the cup, etc.

Then, poets, cease to praise the god,
    And, preachers, cease to strike him,
For, foul or fair, we don't much care,
    We only know we like him;

The more we drink the more we die,
    But why this wordy strife, Sir?
That wine's a curse we don't deny,
    But so is most of life, Sir.

> *Then fill the cup, there's no excuse,*
> *For wine's the devil, wine's the deuce!*
> *Fill, but let me give you warning,*
> *You'll be sorry in the morning.*
> *Wine's a poison, wine's a bane;*
> *Here's good health—and fill again!*

THE SAILOR'S LASS

AIR: "*Now the rosy morn appearing . . .*"

LOVE'S a sad affair, my treasure,
  Ah, to think that we must part!
Still there is a sort of pleasure
  In a badly broken heart;
Ere we sever, you and I,
Let's enjoy a jolly cry.

Ah, my Joe, when you're away
  I'll be wretched, I allow,
I'll be thinking all the day
  "What's my darling doing now?"
In my dreams I'll say your name
And I hope you'll do the same.

When the girls of Bristol City
  Smile upon you, fond and free,
Will you never think them pretty
  But be wishing they were me?
Be they fond and be they fair
Will you wish that I was there?

Kiss me, then. If you forget me
  Mary Jane will droop and die.

Say that you are glad you met me,
   Kiss me quick before I cry.
Fare you well, where'er you be,
God be with you, think of me.

MY SHIP

*(For Captain Slocum, who built a boat with his own
hands and in her sailed round the world, alone.)*

MY ship is my delight,
   And she's the one I woo
When in the shiny night
   We dance across the blue,
With whispering sail and spar
As live as ladies are,
   And twenty times as true.

My ship is my delight,
   I made her, she is mine,
I built her trim and tight,
   I dreamed her gracious line;
No wooden thing is she
But some proud part of me;
   I made her, she is mine.

Then at the helm I stand
   And not alone are we.
Two lovers, hand in hand,
   We ask no company.
So, by some lover's art
I think she knows my heart
   And sings or sighs with me.

SHE-SHANTIES

WHY DOESN'T SHE COME?

Why doesn't she come?
I know we said eight.
Or was it half-past?
That clock must be fast.
Why doesn't she come?
She's ten minutes late.
I'll sit by the door
And see her come in.
I've bought her a rose,
I've borrowed a pin.
I'll be very severe,
I'll tell her, " My dear,
You mustn't be late."
It's a quarter-past eight.
Why doesn't she come?

Why doesn't she come?
This must be the place.
She couldn't forget,
Or is she upset?
Why doesn't she come?
Am I in disgrace?
Oh, well, if it's that,
We were both in the wrong—

I'll give her the rose
And say I was wrong.
I'll give her a kiss
And tell her I'm sorry—
" I'm *terribly* sorry .   ."
Why doesn't she come ?
    Perhaps she is ill—
I fancied last night
Her eyes were too bright—
    A feverish chill ?
She's lying in bed—
She's light in the head !
She's dying—she's dead !
    Why doesn't she come ?

Why doesn't she come ?
    She's tired of me—eh ?
I've noticed a change,
Last night she looked strange.
So this is the end ?
    Why couldn't she say ?
Well, never again !
She needn't explain.
I know who it is—
I know who it is !
I've done with her now.
    Why doesn't she come ?

Why doesn't she come?
It's nearly half-past.
Well, never again!
I'll send her the rose,
I won't say a word,
Just send her the rose—
She'd *laugh*, I suppose!
A flirt and a fraud!
I'll travel abroad;
I'll go to the East;
I'll shoot a wild beast.
And now for a drink,
I'll have a stiff drink—
A brandy, I think—
    And drown myself in it.
I'll shoot myself. . . .   Oh,
How I loved her!——

                              Hul-*lo!*
    What?   LATE?   Not a minute!

WHAT *DO* THE LADIES TALK ABOUT . . . ?

WHEN butlers bring the rich liqueur
    And, stealing from their chairs
With modest eye, discreet and pure,
    The ladies pass upstairs,
Then, while we sling decanters round
    And nurse the frail digestion,
I often to myself propound
    This most improper question—

What do the ladies talk about when the ladies leave the table ?
    The talk, of course, is more refined
    Than that which they have left behind,
    Not there the humour which regales
    The bibulous disgusting males,
      But hose and hat and scarf and sleeve,
      The price of silk and sable—
    This type of thing engrosses Eve.
    No doubt. But still, do YOU *believe*
That's ALL *the ladies talk about when the ladies leave the*
    table ?

That fairy with the marble brow
    Who simpered through the meal,
What topic interests her now ?
    Not politics, I feel.

Those lips that, captivating Earls,
　　Would melt no earthly butter,
Who knows, when she is with the girls,
　　What awful things they utter?

What DO *the ladies talk about when the ladies leave the*
　　table?
　　　　While Thompson o'er the purple cup
　　　　Is tearing reputations up
　　　　His wife, more delicate, no doubt,
　　　　Is flinging compliments about,
　　　　　　Not naughty yarns, but socks and darns
　　　　　　Are exercising Mabel,
　　　　　　And Trade and Education—yes,
　　　　　　And Art of course ; but I can't guess
What ELSE *the ladies talk about when the ladies leave the*
　　table.

For oft when we go up the stair
　　I note the rising blush,
And o'er the animated fair
　　Descends a stealthy hush ;
Ah ! why should maidens fall so mute
　　If previous conversation
Had been concerned with flowers and fruit
　　Or Proportional Representation?

What DO *the ladies talk about when the ladies leave the*
table?
Though ribald laughter rings below,
The drawing-room is nice, we know.
While Mrs. Thompson, sucking sweets,
Is quoting little bits from KEATS,
Her husband tells, with vinous yells,
The stories of the stable.
And what I say is, What a shame!
And, what a sex! But all the same,
What DO *the ladies talk about when the ladies leave the table?*

BUT WILL SHE BE WORTH THE WORRY?

WHENEVER I see a delectable she
   With eyes of a pleasing design
I know that the girl was created for me,
   And I know she will never be mine;
And sly little voices remark in my ear,
   As after the charmer I hurry,
" She is, as you say, a remarkable dear,
   But will she be worth the worry?"

   She will probably wed an attorney instead
      Or be caught by a curate in Surrey;
    Agreed that she seems the adored of your dreams,
     But will she be worth the worry,
               Young man?
    Are you sure she is worth the worry?

And you, if you find you are giving your mind
   To mountains and fountains and forests—
Young man, if you feel a distaste for a meal
   But are constantly seen at the florist's—
If the rest of the race appears prosy and base,
   And you'd like to reside on a star,
If life is a pain till you're with her again
   And, if anything, worse when you are—

Take ship, I implore, to a tropical shore
  And embark on a diet of curry,
For History shows there is danger in does
  And they seldom are worth the worry,
                              No, no !
They NEVER *are worth the worry.*

These sweet pretty things, they may fit us with wings,
  But we fly to the deuce in their talons,
With a casual " Thanks " they will empty our banks
  And go off to a man with a balance ;

In a minute they spoil our devotion to toil,
   They drive us to whisky or worse,
We cease to digest, they rob us of rest,
   And inspire the most terrible verse.

> *But, though this has been the unbroken routine*
>   *Since Helen went off in a hurry,*
> *I know that, as I, you will stoutly reply,*
>   *" Never mind ; they are worth the worry,*
>   *So there !*
>   *They* ALWAYS *are worth the worry."*

SIMPLE SALLY

SIMPLE SALLY hates the city,
   For she loves the open down,
And perhaps it is a pity
   She remains so much in town;

Gentlemen who see her dining,
   Putting caviare away,
Little think that she is pining
   For the heather or the hay;

And this is more surprising still.
When it is time to pay the bill.

"Oh, Mr. Sheep," says Sally with a dimple,
  "P'r'aps a tiny cocktail if you wish;
*You mustn't be extravagant, my tastes are very **simple**;*

Really, nothing more!
  Food is such a bore—
Well, shall we say a little soup and fish?

Something small to follow?
Say a little bird—
Guinea-fowl or swallow,
But a grouse preferred.
Just a little savoury, just a little sweet,
Champagne, if you insist—oh, but nothing more to eat!

Coffee? To be sure.
Ices I adore.
P'r'aps a wee liqueur—
But, really, nothing more!"

Sally, if she could, would wander
  All the day o'er hill and dale,
And perpetually ponder
  Nature and the nightingale;
But instead she stays and roisters
  In her shy reluctant way,
And when young men murmur, " Oysters ? "
  Sally whispers, " What are they ? "
But you should see the waiters grin
When Sally brings a young man in.

" *Oh, Mr. Sheep,*" *says Sally with a dimple,*
  " *You know it's no good asking my advice;*
You mustn't be extravagant, my tastes are very simple.
    Where do people go ?
    I adore Soho,
  But someone said that Claridge's was nice.
    Something à la carte ?
      Naughty Mr. Sheep !
    Plovers' eggs to start ?
      Well, eggs are always cheap.
Then perhaps a play—but does it matter where we sit ?
Stalls, if you insist, but I would just as soon the pit.
    Supper ? If you must—
      Food is such a bore;
    A taxi home, I trust—
      But, really, nothing more ! "

DON'T LET'S GO TO THE DOGS TO-NIGHT

" Come," said he—" a night for dancing,
Lips alight and bright eyes glancing.
        Come ! " the young man cried ;
" Youth should never pause from pleasure,
Fill the cup and trip the measure ! "
        But the girl replied—

" *Don't let's go to the dogs to-night,*
        For mother will be there.
    Auntie chooses all the tunes,
    Uncle bags the best balloons,
    And all the roundest men in town
    Are dancing mother's figure down ;
            Puffing, panting,
            Barging, banting,

129

Bless their snowy hair !
Night-clubs now are simply spas
For our young Methuselahs,
So don't let's go to the dogs to-night
In case my granny's there.

" When I see my oldest aunties
Kicking heels and singing chanties
    Then I have to stop;
All the uncles dance like ladders,
All the aunts are built like bladders
    Just about to pop.

" *Don't let's go to the dogs to-night,*
    For mother will be there.
  When I see the ball-room bulging
  With my ancestors indulging
  Then I've done with Mirth and Mammon.
  Let's go home and play backgammon.

Pushing, shoving,
Lurching, loving,
Bless their silvery hair!
Let the old ones have their fun;
Some day we'll be sixty-one.
But don't let's go to the dogs to-night,
In case my granny's there."

MISS CRINOLINE

I OFTEN wish that I had seen
A real round Miss Crinoline,
So large below, above so lean,
      A pretty contradiction,
In public so subdued an air,
At parties like a polar bear;
But oh, when no Mamma was there,
      Was there the same restriction?

      Miss Crinoline,
      She must have been
          Composed of human clay.
      I'd like to know
      If she was so
          Victorian as they say.

She walked, we read, with dove-like looks,
Tied up with modesty and hooks,
And speaking like JANE AUSTEN's books
      Or DR. JOHNSON's sister;
Oh, did she truly talk like that?
Oh, did she faint and tumble flat
When some young man removed his hat,
      And slap him when he kissed her?

133

Miss Crinoline
Was sound, I ween,
   As any modern belle ;
I think that Miss
Could take a kiss,
   And take it very well.

I think (if there were no one near)
She flung her arms about her dear,
She whispered nonsense in his ear,
   And kissed him sweet and plenty,
And, though those hoops might obviate
An attitude too intimate
I doubt if they were more sedate
   Than naughty 1920.

Miss Crinoline,
She must have been
    As human as her beau ;
What kind of men
Were authors then ?
    Perhaps they didn't know.

Miss Crinoline, come back to us !
There may be awkwardness and fuss
About your entering a bus
    Or bringing off embraces,
But 1926 would see
(If I am right) that one may be
As charming, frolicsome and free,
    And still have all the graces.

Miss Crinoline,
I think, was queen
    Of more than modern arts ;
She kept more hair
Than moderns wear—
    Perhaps she kept more hearts.

BANANA THE BORE

IN a mews behind Mulberry Square
  Was the party to which I was called;
The men were all covered with hair
  And the women were more or less bald;
With her feet on a spongy divan
  And the rest of herself on the floor
I saw what I thought was a man,
  But in fact was Banana the Bore—

Banana the High-brow, Banana the Bore,
With her feet on the sofa, her frame on the floor;
Young poets sat cross-legged and gaped in a row
At the Empress of Chelsea, Princess of Soho,
But I heard what I took for a delicate snore
From the Queen of the High-brows, Banana the Bore.

Her clothes had come over the seas
  From Russia, the Riff or the Rhine,
Her dress was a nightie (Chinese)
  And her shoes of a Spanish design;
She woke and she eyed me askance,
  She hummed an Italian air,
Then sighed that her soul was in France,
  And I wished that her body was there—

Banana the Briton could never abide
The land where the British are forced to reside;
Her English remarks you extract with a wrench,
But she constantly flings you expressions in French,
For the language of SHAKESPEARE is useful no more
When it comes to the thoughts of Banana the Bore.

She has published some verse in her time
    Which was jolly so far as it went;
It lacked only rhythm and rhyme,
    And no one could tell what it meant;
But every intelligent man
    Is sure she could write, if she would,
Some verse which would not only scan
    But be more or less well understood—

Banana, Banana sits mum as a cat;
They say she is deep, and perhaps it is that.
She hasn't much use for the men of her race,
But dig up a Dago and watch the girl's face!
She doesn't like me, as I've hinted before,
And I can't say I dote on Banana the Bore.

'TWAS AT THE PICTURES, CHILD, WE MET

'Twas at the pictures, child, we met,
　Your father and your mother;
The drama's name I now forget,
　But it was like another.

The Viscount had too much to drink,
　And so his plot miscarried,
And at the end I rather think
　Two citizens were married.

But at the opening of the play
　By Fortune's wise design—
It was an accident, I say—
　A little hand met mine.

139

My fingers round that little hand
   Unconsciously were twisted;
I do not say that it was planned,
   But it was not resisted.

I held the hand. The hand was hot.
   I could not see her face;
But in the dark I gazed at what
   I took to be the place.

From shock to shock, from sin to sin
   The fatal film proceeded;
I cannot say I drank it in,
   I rather doubt if she did.

In vain did pure domestics flout
   The base but high-born brute;
Their honour might be up the spout,
   We did not care a hoot.

For, while those clammy palms we clutched,
   By stealthy slow degrees
We moved an inch or two and touched
   Each other with our knees.

No poet makes a special point
   Of any human knee,
But in that plain prosaic joint
   Was high romance for me.

Thus hand in hand and toe to toe,
  Reel after reel we sat;
You are not old enough to know
  The ecstasy of that.

A touch of cramp about the shins
  Was all that troubled me;
Your mother tells me she had pins
  And needles in the knee.

But our twin spirits rose above
  Mere bodily distress;
And if you ask me " Is this Love ? "
  The answer, child, is " Yes."

And when the film was finished quite
  It made my bosom swell
To find that by electric light
  I loved her just as well.

For women, son, are seldom quite
  As worthy of remark
Beneath a strong electric light
  As they are in the dark.

But this was not the present case,
  And it was joy to see
A form as fetching and a face
  Magnetic as her knee.

6

And still twice weekly we enjoy
   The pictures, grave and gross;
We don't hold hands so much, my boy,
   Our knees are not so close;

But now and then, for Auld Lang Syne,
   Or frenzied by the play,
Your mother slips her hand in mine,
   To my intense dismay;

And then, though at my time of life
   It seems a trifle odd,
I move my knee and give my wife
   A sentimental prod.

Well, such is Love and such is Fate,
   And such is Marriage too;
And such will happen, soon or late,
   Unhappy youth, to you.

And, though most learned men have strained
   To work the matter out,
No mortal man has yet explained
   What it is all about.

And I don't know why mortals try:
   But if with vulgar chaff
You hear some Philistine decry
   The cinematograph,

Think then, my son, of your papa,
   And take the kindly view,
For had there been no cinema
   There might have been no you.

I GO ALL GIRLISH WHEN I SEE THE MOON

I CAN'T understand
Why you're holding my hand,
And I feel that I need your advice;

I'm modern, I'm hard,
Soft sentiment barred,
I'm a mixture of acid and ice.
I've done with romantical rot,
I'd rather be high-brow than not

And yet I'm beginning to think,
                          Sir,
I must have a curious kink;

For I go all girlish when I see the moon,
And somebody's playing a sugary tune;
I gaze at the heavenly spheres
With persons who bore me to tears;
I'm soppy and silly
As any young filly,
I giggle and wriggle and swoon.
And when I go girlish and gay
There's no knowing what I may say,
But I always regret it next day,
So don't let us look at the moon!

I'm not one that takes
A fancy to sheikhs,
I belong to the Sensible School;
Though never so tender,
The masculine gender
I spurn as a general rule;
In theory I richly despise
The muscular man with blue eyes,
And in practice I *can't* understand,
                          Captain,
How he comes to be holding my hand.

Why do *I go girlish the moment I see*
A milit'ry officer looking at me?
  I think it is quite on the cards
  I shall marry a man in the Guards,
    Though deep down I hanker
    For some discreet banker—

What can *be the matter with me?*
  For I want to be gloomy and grave,
  But I find that I cannot behave
  When I get tête-à-tête with the brave—
So I hope that you're not a V.C.

My serious side
Is a matter of pride,
I am quite at my best in a slum;
Five days in the week
I work and I speak
For the Blind or the Deaf or the Dumb;
I constantly sing in the choir,
And find all the hymns for the Squire,
And yet now and then and again,
Charles,
Things happen I cannot explain;—

For I go all girlish on Saturday night,
A Saturday seems to unbalance me quite;
I simply will not go to bed,
I want to be fondled and fed,
Though all through the outing
My conscience is shouting,
" Now, Gladys, you know it's not right ! "
And when I go girlish like that
I do things I'm horrified at,
So I'd better go back to the flat,
For I fancy it's Saturday night.

NANNY

I SING a long-neglected dame.
Let plays and poets all proclaim
The wonder of the Mother's name
    And even that of Granny;
Let others tell with loud hurrahs
The general praises of Papas—
I hymn the Mother of Mammas,
    I sing the British Nanny.
Not every pink and girlish thing
    That pushes round a pram,
The ancient rock-like NURSE I sing,
    Britannia's virgin dam,
That, old as mountains and as stout,
From child to child is passed about
Till, childless yet, she passes out,
    The lonely British Nanny.

For she it was that from the first
Refused to judge us by our worst;
We might be yelling fit to burst,
    She crooned a cheerful ditty;
Our very Aunts could not deny
That we were small and ugly fry,
But she with fond prophetic eye
    Maintained that we were pretty.

Alone of all the human race
  She took the kind of view
Of our importance, brain and face,
  That we would have men do;
And I can never quite forget
No other person I have met
Considered me a perfect pet,
  So here's a health to Nanny!

The artless prattle of a child
Drives nearly everybody wild;
And who that for an hour beguiled
  A babe however clever
For all the riches of the rich
Would undertake a life in which
They lived at that exacting pitch
  Ten hours a day for ever?
Though even in the mother's joys
  A grander cycle dawns
When we grow more like little boys
  And less like little prawns,
Our Nanny, in a nobler strain,
Would have us at our worst remain,
A babe for ever pink and plain,
  Herself for ever Nanny.

Alas! the twig becomes a bough;
We do not need a Nanny now;
Forgotten her who showed us how,
  We walk to death or glory;

And whether Fate blows cold or hot,
Whatever women shape our lot,
It's safe to say a Nurse will not
   Be mentioned in the story.
Some other baby far away
   Is hers to soothe or slap,
Some NELSON's in the bath to-day,
   Some SHELLEY in her lap ;
And when I think, on this small star
How many mighty men there are,
I call for wine and drain a jar
   To England's noble Nannies.

MISS BUSY

Miss Busy's my name,
 And I make it my place
To collect and proclaim
 The misdeeds of the race;

From party to party
 I buzz like the bee,
Partaking most hearty
 Of gossip and tea;
I keep a sharp gaze on
 Intrigue and liaison,

152

And over the genial cup
  The good reputations
  Of friends and relations
I tear (very prettily) up :—
    Buzz ! Buzz !
   "Of course you have heard . . .?"
    Buzz ! Buzz !
   "Now, mind, not a word . . .!"

   If you'd know the chief source
    Of a coming divorce,
The name of the villainous He,
   The dates and the places
   Of *all* the embraces,
Apply to Miss Busy the Bee
      Tra-la !

The savages use
  A mysterious trick
To distribute the news,
  And distribute it quick;
But I venture to say
  They can't hold a candle
To the civilised way
  Of distributing scandal.

Young Madam, or Miss,
  Pray take care whom you kiss,
For you may be as sly as an elf,
  But somehow or other
  'Twill get to your mother—
If I have to inform her myself.
    Buzz! Buzz!
  "Mrs. Mole at the play!"

Buzz! Buzz!
"And the Colonel away!"
To-morrow I'll wager
She worships a Major,
On Monday I smell a decree,
On Tuesday she's doping,
On Wednesday eloping,
And I wish she was Busy the Bee
Tra-la!

For it's not that I'm good
I behave in this way.
I'd *like*, if I could,
To be dashing and gay.
I'm neither, but still
One can get, if one cares,
A second-hand thrill
From one's neighbours' affairs.
And while I'm reporting
Each indiscreet courting
However outrageous it be,
Though it shocks me, as such,
I enjoy it as much
As if it had happened to me.
Buzz! Buzz!
"What a dreadful affair . . .!"
Buzz! Buzz!
"But I wish I'd been there . . .!"

For it's wearing, I own,
To be righteous alone,
And, though London with scandal is dizzy,
By general admission
No breath of suspicion
Attaches, alas ! to Miss Busy !
Tra-la!

I WOULDN'T BE TOO LADY-LIKE . . .

I WOULDN'T be too lady-like in love if I were you.
I used to sit in this here park with somebody I knew;
And he was very fond of me, and I was fond of Joe,
And yet we got no forrarder in seven years or so.

> *Well, he'd sit thinking, " Do I dare ? "*
> *And I'd sit thinking, " Lord, he's slow ! "*
> *And so we both sat thinking there,*
> *And then it would be time to go.*
> *I only had to say, " Oh, Joe . . . ! "*
> *And he'd have kissed me, that I know;*
> *But could I do it ? I could not.*
> *And so he married Mabel Bott—*
> *And all because I acted like a lady.*

Some days we used to sit at home and talk about the
   rain;
I've always heard that perfect love made everything
   so plain;
They may be right—all I can say, I never found it so,
For Love is just about the biggest muddle that I know.

Well, dear, he loved me in his way,
And I was very fond of Joe,
But he was too afraid to say,
And I was too refined to show.

And just when things were shaping well
Mamma came in and broke the spell;
It broke his spirit in the end,
He went and found another friend—
And all because I acted like a lady.

I blame it on my mother, dear, who brought me up
    too well,
And told me when a girl was kissed a girl should
    ring the bell.
We women mustn't take the lead, but now and then
    you'll find
It's just as well to give a man a little push behind.

> *Well, he'd sit thinking, " Do I dare ? "*
>   *And I'd sit thinking, " Go it, Joe ! "*
> *And so we just sat thinking there,*
>   *And then, it seemed, he had to go.*
> *I only had to catch his eye,*
> *And sigh a sort of sickly sigh ;*
> *But could I do it ? I could not.*
> *And so he married Mabel Bott—*
>   *And all because I acted like a lady.*

A PAIR OF GLOVES?

PHYLLIS kissed me while I slept
   (Phyllis tells me), none perceiving.
Proof in kind I might accept,
   But the tale is past believing;
For the mortal is not made
   And the monster is not known
But, if those sweet lips be laid
   Light as blossom on his own,
Be his sleep as deep as death
He must feel that fairy breath,
   In his soul will trumpets bellow,
     "Angels kissed me, happy man!"
Phyllis, if your tale were true,
Surely I had dreamed of you!
   I was dreaming, lucky fellow,
     But I dreamed of Ann.
Drowsing in the leather chair,
   Horrid visions filled my mind;
I was hunted by a bear,
   And the bear was close behind.
Sudden, for no certain cause,
   Rapture banished all alarms:
Dodging my pursuer's jaws,
   I was in my darling's arms.

Over the sea we went together
Hand-in-hand, and, oh, what weather!
  Charming Ann could not resist me
    (Which awake, alas! she can).

Phyllis, if your tale is true,
These delights I owe to you;
  I am very glad you kissed me,
    Since I dreamed of Ann.

UNFASHIONABLE FAN

I NEVER cared for Fashion,
    I find a trifle tame
My fellow-creatures' passion
    For looking all the same;
        Let those who please
        Be like two peas,
    But spare your little Fan;
        It pleases me
        To look and be
    As different as I can :—

Let other girls be British—I'm bizarre !
Let other girls look round—I'm ang-u-lar.
        I've eyes like plover's eggs,
        And strange elastic legs,
                Fantastic,
                Elastic,
        Unfashionable Fan.

Whatever is expected
    I do the other thing;
When everyone's dejected
    I clap my hands and sing.
        When So-and-so
        Is all the go,
    At him I snap my thumbs :

162

When vice comes in
I give up sin
And labour in the slums :—

And ev'rybody whispers, " She's unique ! "
When Bridge is quite the thing I play Bezique.
If red's the fav'rite hue
I bound about in blue,
Capricious,
Delicious,
Unfashionable Fan.

I shrink from admiration,
Exhibit now and then
My hearty detestation
Of nice good-looking men ;
But if I see
Some odious He
Who thinks me odious too,
I feel a wish
To land that fish
(And generally do) :—

And all my lovers mutter, " She's bizarre."
Let others look for husbands—I've a car.
And I pity very much
The men who come in touch
With hypnotic,
Exotic,
Unfashionable Fan.

PRIMITIVE PRIM

Miss Primrose looks so soft and sweet
That strangers wager in the street
    She must be took
    From a picture-book
  Of the Period Crinoline;

  Her voice like some shy bird
    Which hopes it won't be heard,
Her eyes are fixed upon her feet
    In case they might be seen.
But deep—deep—deep
    The stream is dark and grim,
And deep within that limpid minx
(Or so at least she fondly thinks)
Is a powerful, passionate, pre-primordial, pagan,
    primitive Prim.

For her no sentimental stuff—
She hoped that men would treat her rough.
  No sugary tune
  About the Moon
  Affected her a bit ;
 In vain was Primrose wooed
 With flowers and fruit and food,

In vain men planned to hold her hand,
  She wanted to be hit.
Ah, deep—deep—deep
  The verdant woods are dim ;
 But then her lovers never guessed
 The furnace in the tender breast
Of pulsing, passionate, pre-primordial, pagan,
  primitive Prim.

At length she met, to her delight,
A man who hated her at sight,
    Though now and then,
    Like complex men,
    He loved her more and more.

His courting ways were queer;
He used to bite her ear,
Or threw, as though his love to show,
          Whole tea-sets on the floor.
And deep—deep—deep
          She loved that forceful Him,
And loved him best when by the hair

He dragged her backwards down the stair,
That palping, passionate, pre-primordial, pagan,
          primitive Prim.

Too late she learned this kind of spouse
Can be a nuisance in the house.
          'Twas not enough
          To treat her rough—
      He knocked the cook about;
      These little habits grow,
      And Prim disliked it so
When Walter to the window flew
          And flung the goldfish out.

Ah, deep—deep—deep
    The slaughtered fishes swim,
And Primrose, I regret to say,
Divorced him in the usual way,
Poor, pulsing, passionate, pre-primordial, pagan,
    primitive Prim.

IT'S A SHAME!

He's knocking me about,
Mrs. Frame ;
He spends his evenings out,
It's a shame !
He's drinking like a fish,
And now and then I wish
He weren't so liverish—
It's a shame !

I'm feeling very queer,
Mrs. Frame ;
Pains in the back, my dear—
It's a shame !
I often sit and think
I might be in the pink
If it wasn't for the drink—
It's a shame !

They say that dogged wins,
Mrs. Frame ;
My girl's expecting twins—
It's a shame !

170

She don't take no advice,
Well, twins is very nice,
But must she have them twice?
　　It's a shame!

This Government's no soul,
　　Mrs. Frame;
They've took me off the dole—
　　It's a shame!

I've got a job, it's true,
But what's it got to do
With BALDWIN if I've *two*?
    It's a shame!

I very much regrets,
    Mrs. Frame,
They mean to tax the bets—
    It's a shame!
Well, if we have to pay
For losing every day,
Where's Magner Carter—eh?
    It's a shame!

To-day I backed a horse,
    Mrs. Frame;
Disqualified, of course—
    It's a shame!
Well, as I said to Fred,
" I back a horse," I said,
" And it's as good as dead "—
    It's a shame!

This Government's no good,
    Mrs. Frame;
They talk of Brotherhood—
    It's a shame!

There's camels in the Zoo
Is better fed than you;
But what does WINSTON do?
      It's a shame!

Oh, well, I always say,
      Mrs. Frame,
We've got to die some day—
      It's a shame!
We'll have another—see?
No, dearie, this is me.
What? Closing? Sure to be!
      It's a shame!

LIFE—OR RATHER LITERATURE

Now Jane loved John, but John loved Ann;
And thus the ghastly thing began.

John married Ann, and so gave pain
To simple, trustful, jealous Jane.

Then John discovered, careless man,
He more or less detested Ann,

While he could not himself contain
When thinking of the lovely Jane.

But Jane meanwhile, impelled by pique,
Had married George the previous week.

(The women met from time to time
And kissed each other.   How sublime !)

John telephoned to Jane one day,
But Ann found out and ran away.

John went to George and told him straight,
" As man to man, I want your mate."

The gentle-minded George agreed
That Fate was very hard indeed,

174

But added he would take the life
Of anyone who took his wife.

John gave up Jane and went away,
But (quite by chance) they met next day.

They met in Sussex, in a mist,
And kissed and kissed and kissed and kissed ;

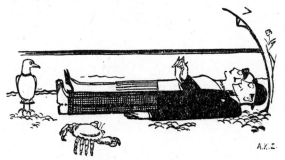

A.K.Z.

Then, passing to a precipice,
They prayed a prayer and kissed a kiss ;

And four miles west of Beachy Head
Their bodies were discovered—dead.

Though lacking, doubtless, in resource,
They took the honourable course.

Poor Ann, repenting of her haste,
Tripped home that day to be embraced,

But, hearing what her John had done,
Had fever and became a nun.

Poor George did not become a monk,
But for the Rockies booked a bunk,

And healed his wounded feelings there
By shooting (more or less) the bear.

Returning with a grizzly's head,
He married someone else instead.

This poem—simple, to be sure—
Contains the whole of Literature;

But rare the writer who confines
Such lots of life in such few lines.

LION AND HORSE

ALL the lions stood a-roaring
  In my Lady Lucy's den,

And you could not see the flooring
  For the literary men ;
Novelists discussed together
Metaphysics and the weather,
  Claret, sandwiches, and sin,

While the painters and musicians
Shyly mentioned their ambitions
    And the women drank it in.
And my Lady Lucy purred
As she prowled about the herd,
" Any person who is not
On the premises is what
Fairly might, I think, be rated as a negligible bird."

Then said Mr. Y. politely,
    " Have you read the works of Horse ? "
Lady Lucy trembled slightly,
    But she answered, " Yes, of course."
Passing on, to one or two
Of the literary Zoo,
    Cornered in convenient nooks,
Cool as cucumber she said
She imagined they had read
    Mr. Horse's jolly books.

And the lions made reply,
Very confident (but shy),
That the works of Mr. Horse
Had considerable force,
But were books which at the present they had not had
    time to buy.

Lady Lucy, looking sickly,
    To her husband sent a note
Bidding him discover quickly
    Who was Horse and what he wrote.
Lord Shalott, the tactful fellow,
In the buffet raised a bellow.

" Who is Horse, and what's he do ? "
" Horse ? Of course ! " said everybody,
" Oh, *you* know ! " said everybody,
 Everybody knew they knew,
Still, they could not place him *quite*.
Did he paint, compose or write ?
Did he etch or win the war ?
What exactly *is* he for ?
And, of course, the strangest question, Why is he not
 here to-night ?

Swiftly spread a dark suspicion—
 Lady L. was out-of-date.
Probably this new musician
 Would be found with Lady Skate.
Lady Tickle keeps the smartest
Kinds of dramatist and artist—
 Ten to one the man was there !
Two by two the guests departed,
Leaving Lucy broken-hearted
 And the Viscount in despair.
As for me, it was the source
Not of malice but remorse,
For I cannot well deny
I was wretched Mr. Y.,
And I know no more than you do of the works of
 Mr. Horse.

°EVERYBODY LOVES ME

WHEN I was quite a tiny mite
Folk fell in love with me at sight;
Old ladies kissed me in my pram
And callers called me Little Lamb;
But Nurse, who had to live with me
And knew me well, did not agree.
And now I have to do with men
I find that things are much as then :—
Everybody loves me, when they come to tea,
But nobody that loves me has to live with me.
Everybody loves me, passionate and strong,
But nobody that loves me loves me very long.

How hard it is to thrust away
A habit formed in childhood's day !
For now, however hard I try,
I seem to catch a caller's eye :
As soon as I have met a man
He wants to kiss me, and he can;
And after that, as you'll agree,
A gentleman should marry me :—
Everybody kisses me, I don't know why,
Everybody loves me, or at least they try.
Everybody's loved me, all my life,
But nobody that loves me wants me for a wife.

Though other girls with icy looks
Can keep a man on tenterhooks,
My lover seems at once to know
How far exactly he can go,
And, having gone as far as that,
Gives me his hand and takes his hat.
Ah, what a wretched girl I am
From too much kissing in my pram!
Everybody loves me, passionate and strong,
But nobody that loves me loves me very long;
Everybody loves me when they come to tea,
But nobody that loves me would like to marry me.

PAINTED PEARL

PAINTED PEARL, I will not kiss you.
    From those lips that scarlet shine
Surely some fell flame must issue
    And infect or frizzle mine.
Darling one, as I have told you,
In my arms I long to hold you,
    But before that fond embrace,
    Darling, will you wash your face?

Though you know my heart is single,
    Not for all the bolts of Jove
Shall my lips with crimson mingle
    Or attempt a mouth that's mauve!
Not for all the whims of Fashion
Will I taste a tinted passion,

183

So, before our first embrace,
Darling, will you wash your face?

Should sad Time your beauty tarnish
    You may paint till all is blue;
Who can blame a coat of varnish
    On a craft no longer new?
But it ought to be unlawful
For a girl to look so awful.
    Pray, before that fond embrace,
    Darling, let me wash your face.

Who would think that virgin kisses
    Slept behind that wanton hue?
Every faded Miss and Mrs.
    Smiles vermilion just like you.
Though you're not, I'm well acquainted,
Half as old as you are painted,
    Tell me, sweet one, if you be
    Twenty-two or thirty-three?

"CHLO"

In Chloe, Lady Portland-Plaice,
You see the regent of the race;
My husband, who has not much brain,
Is in the Cabinet again,
My brothers all are bishops or
Command at least an Army Corps,
My aunts and uncles own the Press—
And I control them, more or less.

> *But in spite of all that,*
> *I'm as gay as a sprat,*
> *And the friskiest fish that I know;*
> *I am known to the mob*
> *As " Topsy" or " Bob,"*
> *While bishops address me as " Chlo."*

Whenever England is at sea
I have the Cabinet to tea;
Prime Ministers look in and hiss,
" What is your view of that or this?"
" Shall Toodles have the Board of Trade?"
" How much should engineers be paid?"
And I reply, " One lump, or two?"
And tell the booby what to do.

By the third or fourth cup
We have fixed the thing up,
And after a sandwich or so
The statesman withdraws
With a burst of applause
For the charm and acumen of Chlo.

I publish every second year
A new account of my career,
For people itch to know the truth
About my short exciting youth ;
The papers pay substantial sums
For my impressions of the slums,
While Balham with Belgravia shares
An interest in my love-affairs.

82

And if everything fails
There are saleable tales
Of political figures I know,
Indiscretions of kings
And the many smart things
That were said to the creatures by Chlo.

My dinner-parties (which I give
But rarely) are superlative ;
I make my husband dine elsewhere,
But everybody else is there—
Prince, poet, politician, Press
(Provided they have evening dress),
And in that scintillating show
None shines so bright as Countess Chlo.

Archbishops I shock,
Ambassadors rock
At the tiniest threat of a mot,
While many a peer
Dines out for a year
On a single quotation from Chlo.

To every charitable aim
I gladly give at least my name ;
If it will help in any way
I will be photographed all day,

If necessary, take the Chair
And let them photograph me there.
Indeed, when I am dead and gone,
I doubt if England can go on.

> *And, though now and again*
> *I may suffer from strain,*
> *It's a great satisfaction to know*
> *That Britain would stop*
> *With an audible pop*
> *If an accident happened to Chlo.*

I'M SO GLAD HE LOVES ME FOR MY BRAINS

SOME girls I know would rather they
    Were beautiful than clever,
But beauty's brief, I always say,
    While wisdom lasts for ever;
And that's the reason I respeck
    My man-friend in the City
Who loves me for my intelleck
    And not because I'm pretty.

Oh, I'm so glad he loves me for my brains!
* For what is charm without intelligence?*
*   It's not so much my eyes*
*   That Albert seems to prize;*
* What staggers him is my artistic sense.*
And every time he kisses me he says a bit from TENNYSON
* So I'm quite sure he loves me for my brains.*

It's funny, not so long ago
  My intelleck was pitied;
My friends have even called me slow,
  My family, half-witted;
But now it seems I've quite a head
  And have no cause to grovel—
Why, many gentlemen have said
  I ought to write a novel.

And I'm so glad they love me for my brains!
  Somehow it improves the whole position.
      It's not my face or form
        That makes Sir William warm,
  But, oh! he does admire my intuition!
And every time he kisses me he says it's quite platonic-like,
  So then I know he loves me for my brains.

Then everyone is kind indeed
   About my education;
My Albert brings me books to read,
   Which helps the conversation;
And really it is rather fine
   How often we discover
That I am like the hero-ine
   And he is like the lover.

Oh, I'm so glad they love me for my brains!
* It's much more satisfact'ry, I should say;*
*   I never knew Sir John*
*   What I call carry on,*
* Excepting in an intellectual way;*
And every time he sees me home he says a piece of poitry,
* So then I know he loves me for my brains.*

CLOSE-UPS

THE reigning queen of film and screen,
　　It is my special art
With nose and eye to signify
　　The feelings of the heart;
With each emotion in its place
　　The public mind I touch,
Amazed that such a little face
　　Can register so much :—

'Tis evening.　Rose her time employs
In brooding o'er her childhood's toys,
　　　She longs, in vain,
　　　To see again
　　Her little nursery chum;
　　　Fond memories race
　　　Across her face,
And Love, and Tedium;

Sweet longings for the Might-Have-Been,
    And Passion, mixed with Pique,
While tears of molten glycerine
    Steal softly down her cheek.

Then, Heavens ! up dashes
    The clean-living boy ;
With fluttering lashes
    I register Joy,

While, coy but not churlish,
    My bosom doth swell,
And registers girlish
    Confusion as well.

But see ! he drops a letter, which
    I eagerly peruse !
He loves a widow, who is rich
    And meets him in a Mews.

Am I defeated ?   Not at all.
I feature Jealousy and Gall.
I lose my grip.   I go and get
Entangled with a wicked set,
Take lots of drugs, and drink and bet,
    And pawn my underclothing ;
A Marquis, in an aeroplane,
Attempts my honour, but in vain,
For here I register Disdain,
    Pride, Purity, and Loathing.
I set my teeth, for far beneath
The Boat-train speeds for France,
And Hector, by a happy chance,
    Is standing on the top.
Beside me still the noble brute
Is pressing his detested suit,
So, opening a parachute,
In Hector's arms I drop !

My lips are still set,
For I cannot forget
    The man is concealing
      His love for Another ;
But oh, you can trace
The remorse in my face
    On Hector's revealing
      The widow's his mother !
The bells are soon pealing—
    " Love's Temple of Bliss "—
And (probably kneeling)
    We register Bliss.

POLITICS;

Or, "I've Done with Lloyd George"

Well, I said to Fred, Mrs. Higgins, in "The
    Blackbird,"
    "This here Government gets a feller's goat."
Fred said, "You're right, Bert; but then it stands to
    reason,
    Nothing's been the same since the women had the
    vote."
        Well, then we had one,
        And then we had another;
    Fred stood Bottletop and I stood Fred,
    And "Say what you like, Mr. Bottletop," I said,
        "I've done with Lloyd George."

Then I said, chivalrous, "It isn't only women."
    Fred said, spirited, clearing of his throat,
"Believe me or not, Bert, I never backed a winner,
    Not since the perishing women had the vote!"
        Well, then we had one,
        Then we had another,
        And then we had another one,
        And after that another;

Fred stood Bottletop and I stood Bill,
And I said, " Well, boys, say what you will,
   I've done with Lloyd George."

Then Bill said, warm-like, " Say that again, Fred ! "
   Fred yelled " Certainly ! " taking off his coat ;
" If you want my opinion of the influence of women,
   Nothing's been the same since the women had the vote ! "

So Bill fetched Fred one,
I fetched him another,
In came a constable,
Up came another ;
Bill got one month
And I got another,
And all for a talk about politics with Fred.
But " Say what you like, Mr. Magistrate," I said,
" I've done with LLOYD GEORGE."

THE PROPOSAL

(Old Style)

He. Lovely Phyllis, marry me,
Vile, unworthy though I be.
Though I have not gold or grace,
Scarcely fit your shoes to lace,
Though you might as likely wish
Marriage with a frog or fish,
Share my life,
Be my wife,
Will you marry me—Yes or No?

She. Sir, you take me by surprise.
See, I faint !   My colour flies !
In my simple girlish heart
Thoughts of marriage play no part.
Oh, Sir, oh ! I never guessed
This was why my hand was pressed !
No, Sir, no ;
I don't know
If I'll marry you—Yes or No?

He. I shall wait, then, I shall speak
In this fashion once a week ;

Age shall not my suit foreclose,
Toothless I shall still propose,
And upon my death-bed lie
Till they bring me your reply;
    As I die,
      Still shall sigh,
  Will you marry me—Yes or No?

She. Be not hasty, dangler dear,
Dangle yet another year.
Be my friend, Sir, fetch my fan,
Send me flowers when you can;
But these frenzies pray defer,
Let me be a sister, Sir;
      Passion, hence!
      Have some sense,
  Be my brother, Sir—Yes or No?

He. Phyllis, I have sisters four
And I do not ask for more;
But at last, like ships that rest
Pillowed on their tyrant's breast
So, sweet cyclone, do I mean
In your heart to float serene.
      Sister? Fudge!
      I'll not budge!
  Will you marry me—Yes or No?

She. George (if I may call you that),
        Now my heart goes pit-a-pat,
        For this moment, while you spoke,
        What no doubt is Passion woke ;
        Though till now I never knew,
        I believe I dote on you ;
                Love unguessed
                Filled my breast,
        I will marry you—Yes, Sir, yes !

THE PROPOSAL

(New Style)

Don't you think I mean to dangle
  At yours heels, my dearest dear,
Fetch your fan and find your bangle,
  Offer marriage once a year !
I won't wait till I am weary,
  Always true and always there !
You don't want a lover, dearie,
  But a good Commissionaire.
      Yes or No !
      Or off I go—
  And I don't come back, my darling !

If you don't want ME,
  You'll have to get another !
For I won't be
  No little girl's brother.
I won't fetch and carry
  Like a puppy for a bone,
I want for to marry,
  And I've sisters of my own.
I don't care much for the Plato touch,
  And I won't be nobody's poodle !

" Why do people want to kiss you ? "
    What's it got to do with you ?
That's a very minor issue—
    All that matters is, they do.
Conversation's not my sport,
    Concerts give me horrid pains ;
He-Man Harry—that's my sort,
    And red the red blood in rrv veins :—
            So, Yes or No,
            Or off I go,
    And I don't come back, my darling !

    If you don't want ME,
        You'll have to do without me.
    There don't seem to be
        No chivalry about me ;
    I love you, Lizzie,
        But you'd better understand,
    I don't go dizzy
        When you let me kiss your hand,
    I'm He-Man Harry, I want for to marry,
    And I won't be nobody's poodle !

CLINGING NANCY

They call me Clinging Nancy
  (Although my name is Jane),
And just because when I am kissed
I seldom wrestle or resist,
I do not roar and run for life,
I do not wail, " I am a wife ! "
  But if he takes my fancy
    I cry, " Kiss me again."

What puzzles me is this—
  Why husbands make a fuss
About a tiny kiss.
  It is preposterous.
What if the booby misses
A hundred thousand kisses ?
  I can at once restore
  A hundred thousand more.

They call me Clinging Nancy
  (Oh, is it not a shame ?),
For why, if someone needs a kiss,
Should someone else begrudge him this
When I can make a million more
Exactly like the one before ?
  I never, never can see
    Why I should be to blame.

When gentlemen take my hand
  And shake it hard and long
In all this virtuous land
  No creature calls it wrong.
Then why should they make faces
At much more brief embraces ?
  For what's a kiss or two
  But a nice quick " How d'ye do ? "

They call me Clinging Nancy
  (Although my name is Jane),
For when I'm kissed I seldom yell
Or rush about and ring the bell ;
I cannot raise a tiny shriek,
I do not slap the villain's cheek,
  But if he takes my fancy
    I cry, " Kiss me again."

LOVE IN THE NATIONAL GALLERY

Most lovers in London have found
   There is nowhere for lovers to go ;
One look, and a crowd gathers round,
   And to-morrow the papers will know ;
But still, if they want to embrace,
   For persons of tact and good sense
There is many a suitable place
   Maintained at the public expense.

And that's how I loved Mr. Mallory ;
We met in the National Gallery,
But I did not think much of his salary,
   And so I dismissed the poor man.

But now, when I see an Old Master,
My heart beats a little bit faster,
> *For it may have been WATTEAU*
> *Or jolly old GIOTTO,*
But that's where our passion began.

My mother's the difficult sort,
   And he'd a mamma of his own,
And so we were able to court
   At the Public Collections alone.
Ah ! many the vows that we swore
   And many the kisses he took
As we sat with one eye on the door
   And the other on " Crossing the Brook " !

And oh, how I miss Mr. Mallory !
We kissed in the National Gallery,
And but for my sad shilly-shallery
  I ought to have married the man.

I tell you, I shake like a jelly
When I look at a good Botticelli,
    For we met as a rule
     In the Florentine School,
And that's where our passion began.

  Then I found, with my friend Mr. Watts,
    The British Museum delicious,
  And we studied Phœnician pots
    Till people became quite suspicious.
  We went to South Kensington too,
    And oft we have told the fond tale
  Behind a stuffed shark that he knew,
    Or safe in the shade of the whale.

And then there was dear Mr. Rose,
Who kissed me at Madame TUSSAUD'S

He was constantly blowing his nose,
  And so I dismissed the poor man.
But often my little heart throbs
When I think of Lord NELSON or HOBBS
      It was just between those
      That I kissed Mr. Rose,
And that's where our passion began.

  But now that I'm married to Watts,
    Museums don't play the same part;
  I'm tired of Phœnician pots,
    But I still have a passion for Art.
  Mr. Watts is quite jealous, I find,
    But he can't have the smallest objection
  To a person improving her mind
    At the TATE or the WALLACE Collection.

For oh, how I miss Mr. Mallory!
We meet at the National Gallery;
I don't like to think of his salary,
  For now he is earning such lots.
I'm tired of Phœnician pots,
For that's where I met Mr. Watts;
      But oh! how I thrill
      To a Gainsborough still,
For that's where I meet Mr. Mallory.

SONG FOR A GENTLEMAN ON A COMMON
OCCASION;

OR, TACTFUL REPLY TO A NEW LOVE ON HER REFERRING INDELICATELY TO SOME OF THE OLD

Ah, call me not inconstant, who
Am constantly in love with two !
We know the frowns of Heaven fall
On him that never loves at all,
From which it follows, does it not ?
That he is best who loves a lot ;
And so, my love, look not so blue—
I am too good to be quite true.

Who does not hate a narrow mind
By one unchanging creed confined ?
So do I shun with every art
A too precise and narrow heart.
Though by the stars I may have sworn
That Alice was the fairest born,
No bigot, owned that I was wrong
The moment Lucy came along.

Sweet Cupid fits the soul with wings
And lifts us up to higher things,
The heart more generous and the mind
To new nobilities inclined.
I never fail, when love begins,
For ever to renounce my sins ;
And nothing can be quite in vain
That makes a man reform again.

And pray, what chemist rests content
With one unproved experiment ?
Does he not turn from test to test,
And through the better find the best ?

So I that swore, high optimist,
A faultless woman must exist.
My trials done, triumphant see
The perfect model, dear, in thee.

And think not they who ne'er did kiss
Embrace the better, sweet, for this.
You do not trust that plumber more
Who swears he never plumbed before,
Nor in the battle choose your knight
From them that never fought a fight.
I could not love thee, dear, so well
Had I not first loved Isabel.

MRS. MOLE

" THIS is the garden.   I can see
You're fond of gard'ning—so are we.
A pity it is winter still,
You ought to see our daffodil.
We had some snowdrops in this bed,
I wish you'd seen them, but they're dead ;
And in this other one we grow
Those What-d'-you-call-'em's in a row,
Of course you know the ones I mean,
Such pretty flowers, red and green—
Well, not exactly red, but pink,
Some funny foreign name, I think,
You know, they have those pointed leaves,
Not *Cattlecrop*, not *Widows' Eaves*,
Not *Alpigloss*, not *Bishop's Hat*,
But something similar to that—
I've got it !   *Poly-something Pride !*
No, those are on the other side.
Well, did you ever ?   What a shame !
I never do forget a name.
Well, anyhow, it's there they grow,
And really it's a splendid show,
You cannot think how fine they are !
Don't put your foot in that—it's tar.

And in this pond Tom keeps his newts,
The most attractive little brutes !
Of course, they won't come out to-day,
You'll have to come again in May.
Last Whitsuntide we had a frog,
But it was eaten by the dog.

" And here we have the tennis-court,
It's narrow, yes, and rather short ;
But still it is the same for all—
The Vicar says he *likes* it small.

You're sure you're not too tired, my dear ?
We mean to put the chickens here.
But if we put the chickens there,
The hammock has to go elsewhere ;
You see the difficulty, dear ?
We've always had the hammock here.
Of course, it isn't used a lot,
We have the hammock when it's hot.

They say that chickens must have air,
And so we couldn't put them *there*.
You see, whichever way one tries,
It's awkward—what do *you* advise?
I think we'll put the hammock *here*.
You'll tell me when you're tired, my dear?

" Yes, that's my Milly, playing scales.
We suffer very much from snails.

It's odd we have so many more
Than Mrs. Hickory next-door.
I dare say Algernon is right—
She throws them over in the night.
I shouldn't be surprised—would you?
It's wonderful what people do.
My neighbour on the other side
Has just committed suicide.

A pity.   Such a pleasant man !
We used to share a watering-can.
There'll be an inquest, I suppose.
And now I'll have to buy a hose.
That's our laburnum.   That's a pear.
It's pretty, but it doesn't bear.
Now tell me, which do you prefer,
The smell of mint, or lavender ?

I never know.   They're both so sweet.
We have the two.   It's quite a treat.
What, going, dear ?   Not tired, I trust ?
Well, if you must, of course you must.
A pity.   For you ought to see
My Milly imitate a bee.
But tell me, dear, before you go,
Can you get arrowroot to grow ?
It wants a gravel soil, they say.
I've tried and tried.   But this is clay.

The hens will be a worry too.
I really don't know *what* to do.
You see the difficulty, dear?
We've *always* had the hammock here.
I doubt if Algernon could bear
To see the hammock over there.
But there it is. One has to change.
But still, it will seem *very* strange.
Do say you haven't walked too far.

Mud on your skirt? No, dear, it's tar.
And there's a little on your hat!
How ever did you manage that?
Oh, well, a little turpentine—
You see? there's not a drop on mine.
Yes, isn't it a pretty hall?
I am so glad you liked it all.
Good-bye, my dear. Somehow I knew
That you were fond of gardens too.

It's raining, yes.   Excuse me, dear,
You have some tar behind the ear.
Yes, that's the way—across the stile—
And then the tram is half a mile.
Yes, you'll be home in half a tick,
You'll miss the thunder if you're quick.
Good-bye !   *Good*-bye !   Now come again !
Of course, if you are off to Spain,
You'll miss the garden.   Anyhow,
You've seen a little of it now.
But still, it's never quite the same
Without the flowers.   Glad you came.
Well, that's for dinner.   I must fly !
Good-bye again.   *Good*-bye !   Good-bye ! "

WHAT'S ALL THIS TALK ABOUT LOVE?

NOWADAYS,
In books and plays,
Love, it seems, is quite a craze.
Really, anyone would say
To see our modern dramas
The upper-classes spent the day
In passion and pyjamas.

But what's all this talk about Love?
Have we no worthier topics
Than furtive embraces
At watering-places,
Or dusky intrigues in the Tropics?
Well, look at myself—I'm as bright as a bee,
But no problems of passion preoccupy ME,
For what with my cats and Committees, you see,
I haven't a moment for Love.

On the stage,
In youth and age,
Wet or fine, emotions rage;
But in life we make less fuss
About the crude affections,
And what the village does discuss
Is cows and their complexions.

So what's all this talk about Love?
  It's just a theatrical fashion,
    Take my own case—
    I'm the life of the place,

But I haven't a moment for passion.
Well, look at my Mondays—an average day—
The Glee-club, the Scouts, AND *the* Y.M.C.A. *!*
But we never see that side of life in a play—
  What IS *all this talk about Love?*

You don't see me
In *déshabille*
Behaving tenderly at tea.
A woman has enough to do
To keep the parish going
And make the Vicar number Two
Without the Vicar knowing.

What's all this talk about Love?
I'm Colonel-in-Chief of the Guides,
On several Committees
For cleansing our cities,
And frequently lecture, with slides ;
So with this and with that, and the garden, you see,
No problems of passion preoccupy ME,
Yet my life is as full as a woman's can be——
What IS *all this talk about Love ?*

UP, GENTLEMEN—THE LADIES!

A TOAST

(And a humble offering to after-dinner speakers)

PEACE, politicians ! pray forbear,
    We've slept through six orations ;
Let Beauty's health be now our care,
    And hang the health of nations !
If you have sweetheart, wife or niece,
Then charge a glass (or two) apiece,
And every man stand up who can—
    Up, Gentlemen—the Ladies !

Though in these murky modern days,
    When Youth knows what is what, Sir,
When Oxford struts about in stays
    And Lady Dash does not, Sir,
Boys will be girls and women men—
And who can swear to cock or hen ?—
Still, one may say in a general way
    Up, Gentlemen—the Ladies !

Now powder decks Sir Galahad
  And smoke surrounds Elaine, Sir,
And nobody is good or bad
  But psychic or insane, Sir,
And skirts are brief and trousers bold,
And Youth is sadly young, we're told;
But that's a tale that's very old—
  So, Gentlemen—the Ladies !

Though high and low allure, we know,
  The rich are not the ripest ;
To Ascot for the Fashions go,
  For Beauty to the typist ;
But beauty's not the only charm,
The plainest countess means no harm,
So, fair or not, salute the lot—
  Up, Gentlemen—the Ladies !

The Parties bark and scratch and bite,
    And by an implication
That black is black or white is white
    One risks a conflagration.
This toast (of which I've said enough)
Is less inflammatory stuff;
Non-party now, we make our bow,
    United, to the Ladies !

In every club I hear it said—
    I have it from a Dean, Sir—
That England, if not wholly dead,
    Is not what she has been, Sir.
I am not much concerned, because
It's my belief she never was.
And now, I think, it's time to drink—
    Up, Gentlemen—the Ladies !

PLAIN JANE

I LIKE THEM FLUFFY

SOME like them gentle and sweet,
  Some like them haughty and proud,
Some of us like them petite,
  And some of us love the whole crowd;
Some will insist upon grace,
  And some make a point of the pelf,
But, to take a particular case,
  I do like them fluffy myself:

I like them fluffy, I freely confess,
With fluffy blue eyes and a fluffy blue dress,
  With fair fluffy hair, like Love-in-a-mist,
  And lips that declare "I want to be kissed";
    With fluffy soft cheeks, like plums on a wall,
    With a fluffy soft heart—and no brains at all.

Some like a girl that's well read,
  Some like a shingle or crop,
But I don't care what's in her head,
  If there's plenty of hair on the top.
Give me the frivolous locks,
  Give me the Gaiety Queen,
Give me the Chocolate Box,
  And give me the Girls' Magazine!

231

I like them fluffy—I know it's bad taste—
With fluffy soft looks and a flower at the waist,
  With golden hair flying, like mist round the moon,
  And lips that seem sighing,"You must kiss me soon,"
    Not huffy, or stuffy, not tiny or tall,
    But fluffy, just fluffy, with no brains at all.

Brains are all right in their place,
  But oh, it's a shock to the heart
If the lady postpones an embrace
  To enquire your opinions on Art!
And to-day, as I paused on the brink,
  I own I was slightly annoyed
When she sighed and said,"What do you think
  Of the basic assumptions of FREUD?"

" I like them fluffy," I gently replied,
" Not huffy, or stuffy, or puffy with pride,
  With downy soft eyebrows and artful blue eyes,
  The kind that the highbrows pretend to despise,
    With fluffy complexions, like plums on a wall,
    And fluffy opinions, and no brains at all."

233

THE PROLETARIAT

I WAS playing darts in the old *Blue Dragon*,
  There was young Bert Baxter and a little friend
      of Jane's,
Harriet and Albert, that works on the railway,
  And old Bill Mortimer that works upon the drains;
When up jumps a lunatic and starts a little chat,
And he calls us " Members of the Proletariat!"

> *Oh, we* did *laugh!*
> *Oh, we* did *laugh!*
>   *Ha! Ha! Ha!*
> *Well, it knocks a fellow flat!*
> *And I said : "Well, boys, what d' you think of that?*
> *Fancy me a member of the Proletariat!*
>   *Fancy me and you,*
>   *And Harriet and Hugh,*
>   *All these years, boys, and, Lord, we never knew*
> *We was all life-members of the Proletariat,*
> *The Proly-oly-roly-poly-proly-tari-at!"*

Well, I said, " Long words never lined a breadbox,
  But a nice long word is a comfort, all the same;
You can say what you like about the language of
      Shakespeare,
  But this here mouthful puts the man to shame.
For you do feel good, and there's no denying that,
If you speak about a plumber as the Proletariat!"

Oh, we did laugh!
Oh, we did laugh!
Ha! Ha! Ha!
Well, it knocks a fellow flat!
And Bill said, firm-like, he didn't mean to be
Not an economic pawn, nor a bond-slave—see?
So I held Nell's hand,
And we all felt grand,
And we give three cheers for to Socialise the Land,
And we took a season-ticket for the Proletariat,
The Proly-oly-roly-poly-proly-tari-at!

Then I went out, and I said to a policeman,
  "Comrade, Wage-slave, ain't it very strange,
These here capitalists don't want to nationalise
    The means of Production, Distribution, and
      Exchange?
If you ask me, Constable, I'm taking off my hat
To the Nancimancipation of the Proletariat!"

Oh, he did laugh!
Oh, he did laugh!
Ha! Ha! Ha!
Well, it knocks a fellow flat!
So he said, kind-like, " Come along of me!"
But I said, " What about Solidaritee?"
And Bill said " Shame!
Solidarity's the game!"
But he took me off to the station, just the same,
Though we're both life-members of the Proletariat,
The Proly-oly-roly-poly-proly-tari-at!

THE FIVE-O'CLOCK FAIRIES

AT five o'clock and after,
  Down every City street,
You'll hear their elfin laughter,
  You'll hear the fairy feet.
Cheapside seems full of roses,
  The pavement rocks with fun,
As, powdering their noses,

From bank and shop they run——

Homeward, hurrah!
Go the Five-o'clock Fairies,
  Hurrying, scurrying,
    Home to Mamma.
What fairy red hats
    And fairy pale faces,
What stockings and spats
    And vanity cases!
London's in flower,
  The Bank is a bower,
And constables bud to the best of their power,
  While, since it's our duty
    To venerate Beauty,
I take off my hat to the Five-o'clock Fairies.

Why are these dull photographers
  In Lady Dash engrossed
When I know ten stenographers
  Would leave her at the post?
A fig for your New Yorkers!

Your midinettes—pooh, pooh!
Madrid may hold some corkers—
Well, we have one or two.

  Homeward, hooray!
Go the Five-o'clock Fairies,
 Cantering, bantering,
  Into the fray!
Fighting for trams
  And battling for buses—
What jostles and jambs!
  What fairy-like cusses!
Caught in the rain,

 Crushed in the train,
Up at six-thirty to do it again,
 Tough as they're tender,
 They never surrender——
I take off my hat to the Five-o'clock Fairies.

You ladies rich and splendid,
  If you have ever been
Locked in some space intended
  For one not large sardine,
Give thanks you travel gaily,
  Not as the fairies do,
Who fight their passage daily
  From Cannon Street to Kew.

Homeward again
Go the Five-o'clock Fairies,
  Wearily, drearily,
    Into the train.
Jolly stockbrokers
    Have got the last places,
And prosperous smokers
    Blow smoke in our faces,

Rolling and reeling,
So faint we are feeling,
But stockbrokers never get out before Ealing.
And the same thing to-morrow—
To-morrow—to-morrow!
I take off my hat to the Five-o'clock Fairies.

SHE LOVES ME—SHE LOVES ME NOT——

HE.

She loves me? She loves me not?
It's very hard to say.
She loves me not this evening,
She loved me yesterday.
She loves me in the blue dress,
She hates me in the grey.
She loves me? She loves me not?
She loves me not . . .

I've been sitting here with Phyllis
Picking petals off the lilies—
    Picking petals off the roses
    In the good old way;
I've been sitting here since lunch
Wrecking roses by the bunch,
    And I doubt if I proposes
        For they all say "Nay!"

She loves me—she loves me not . . .
  There's something in her eye,
Is it welcoming or warning?
  Is it cynical or shy?
If I kissed her very gently
  Would she cling or would she cry?
She loves me?   She loves me not?
  She loves me not . . .

SHE.

What's he thinking of, I wonder?
Have I made some fatal blunder?
  Am I very, very boring?
    Heaven only knows.
Should I be a little bolder?
Shall I turn the chilly shoulder?
  Is he angry or adoring?
    I shall ask this rose . . .

He loves me?   He loves me not?
  This booby of a man—
He loves me not?   He loves me?
  Is it me or is it Ann?
He loves me—will he kiss me?
  If he wants to, well, he can.
He loves me?   He loves me not?
  He loves me not?   He loves me!

HE.

Not a word.   What is she thinking?
Is it sentiment or shrinking?
If a gentleman proposes
    Will she faint with fright?
Will she never, never utter?
I'm about as brave as butter,
    But I'll go on wrecking roses
        Till it comes out right . . .

She loves me?   She loves me not?
    It's very hard to tell.
She loves me?   If I kissed her
    Would she run and ring the bell?
If I kissed her very gently,
    Would she kiss me very well?
She loves me?   She loves me not?
    She loves me not . . .

She loves *me!*

START HER ON CHAMPAGNE, BOY . . .

START her on champagne, boy, but break her in to
    hock—
That's the only rule of life that's steady as a rock.
I've seen so many promising entanglements decline
'Cos the lady weren't contented with a nice still wine.

Start her on champagne, boy, but break her into
    hock;
And the longer you leave it the bigger is the shock.
    I used to say to Liz,
      " Now, what about some fizz?
     Or shall we have a nice glass of hock?"
I told her the history, the mystery of hock,
I told her that hock would go sweetly with her
    frock,
How the felon at the block as a rule demanded
    hock,
    And other things with which I needn't trouble
     'ee;
And " Hock," said she, " would do very well
    for me";

And I said, " Waitah! a bottle of 53!"
And then, I don't know why—
Was it something in her eye?—
In a minute I'd be ordering the bubbly.

If a lady chooses lobster when there's plaice at one-
and-ten
It's a strain upon the passions of the tenderest of men.
Give her dinner *à la carte* when your romance has just
begun,
But if love is to be lasting stick to *table d'hôte*, my
son.

Start her in the stalls, boy, but train her to

the pit;

Educate them up until they don't care where they sit.
I've done with Lizzie, boy,
For her tastes were too Savoy,
And mine were more Soho, I must admit.

I told her of the cooking and the quaintness of Soho,
I told her to Soho all the clever people go,
I told her that Soho was the haunt of the beau
And the beginning of innumerable marriages;
And "Soho!" she'd declare, "I'll be happy anywhere,"
And I'd say, "Splendid! Well, a bus goes there";

And then, I don't know why—
Was it something in her eye?—
We'd be driving in a motor-cab to Claridge's.

MY OLD HOT-WATER-BOTTLE

No, Mr. Nibbs, I never thought of marriage—
   At least, I never thought of it again;
It's not the institution I disparage,
   It's just the thought of Woman gives me pain.

> *Give me my old hot-water-bottle,*
>   *And you can keep your wives.*
> *Love comes and goes, as well I knows,*
>   *But this old pal survives.*
> *A woman, so the poet sings,*
> *Can raise the soul to better things;*
> *And so she may, but all I say*
>   *Is, " Give me my old hot-water-bottle."*

Early or late, when I come home she's waiting,
   Early or late, she never says a word;

She never doubts the story I'm relating,
  She never even asks me what occurred.

> *Give me my old hot-water-bottle,*
>   *Red flannel round it put,*
> *And let it lie and gurgle by*
>   *My lonely little foot.*
> *That's all the comfort that I want*
> *When I've had too much crême de menthe—*
> *A loving wife can shape one's life,*
>   *But give me my old hot-water-bottle.*

My faithful friend, could you and I be parted?
  When I am gone, whose bottle will you be?
Could I endure to know that you had started
  Warming the toes of some detested she?

> *Give me my old hot-water-bottle*
>   *Before I make my will,*
> *And let me clasp at my last gasp*
>   *The good red flannel still;*
> *And when I reach my long last bed,*
> *Strew no sad flowers o'er my head,*
> *But, nice and neat, lay at my feet*
>   *Alice, my old hot-water-bottle.*

SUSAN GOES SHOPPING

WHEN Susan goes shopping
   There's joy in the town,
The weather is topping,
   The Bank-rate goes down;
Policemen, seraphic,
   Extend their blue arms,

Obstructing the traffic
  To study her charms;
The prosiest grocer
Contrives to come closer,
The fishmongers yearn at their doors;

The shopwalker rushes
To meet her and blushes
As soon as she enters the Stores.
  And all of them say,
  " Dear Moddam! Good-day!
  Moddam! Moddam!
  Beautiful Moddam!
What do you fancy to-day?
  It's perfectly topping
  To see you out shopping!
  We've all kinds of raiment,
  But don't think of payment—
Just take what you fancy away."

She's rather fastidious;
   She tries on a shoe;
The first one is hideous,
   The second won't do.
They ransack the cellar
   And bring her some more,
Which seem to repel her
   As much as before.
Till, lost in a litter
Of shoes that don't fit her,
And footwear enough for a ball,
   She murmurs, " Don't worry;
   There's really no hurry;
I don't want a shoe after all."

And all of them say,
" Sweet Moddam! Hooray!
Moddam! Moddam!
Beautiful Moddam!
We're anxious to meet your desires.

Please go on shopping,
Keep changing and chopping;
We've everything handy,
From buttons to brandy,
But what is it Moddam requires?"

She's not very certain—
   They show her a cheese,
A hat and a curtain,
   A jolly chemise,

And ribbons and laces,
   And cloth by the mile.
Controlling their faces,
   But failing to smile,
They clamber up ladders,
   And, genial as adders,
Surround her with satin and silk,
   Until she confesses,
     " I've plenty of dresses,
But I *should* like a glass of hot milk."

And all of them say,
" Sweet Moddam! Good-day!
Moddam! Moddam!
Beautiful Moddam!
We wish you were stopping
    A fortnight or two.
Pop in when you're popping,
Keep changing and chopping,
Go on till we're dropping,
    We've nothing to do;
But if these researches
Don't lead to a purchase,
We'd like to stop shopping,
    Dear Moddam. Would you?"

I WILL BE BOHEMIAN, I WILL . . .

I LIKE this party,
                    I do,
I feel so Arty,
                    Don't you?
My, it's a wonderful sight,
So many people who write,

So many actors
And concert attractors—
I do feel Bohemian to-night!

And I will be Bohemian, I will!
I'll talk about Art till I'm ill;
On my stomach I'll lie
And discuss ROGER FRY—
I will be Bohemian, I will!

So this is Bohemia,
Old boy?
Is it nervous anæmia,
Or joy?
Who are the ladies who cook
Haddock and eggs in a nook?
What are they called,
And why are they bald,
And are they as odd as they look?

Make me Bohemian, I beg!
Give me a haddock and egg!
And what is the man
Who is using a fan,
And why does he stand on one leg?

Ain't the discussion
          Bizarre?
Golly! How Russian
          We are!

And Olga Popolga's divine,
And if she declines to be mine
    I'll try to look Tchehov
    And shatter the neck of
A bottle of strawberry wine.

For I will be Bohemian, I will!
I'll gobble up Life till I'm ill;
    I'll double my ration
    Of gaspers and Passion—
I will be Bohemian, I will!

No more Convention
                For me !
I'll fearlessly mention
                The flea.
And we'll have a studio too,
I'll whitewash the wallpaper blue,
        And make no more strictures
        On Futurist pictures,
Whatever the horrors you do ;

But if you paint eyelashes green
I'll murmur, " I see what you mean,"
        And express no surprise
        At rectangular thighs ;
I will be Bohemian, old bean !

Life is so jolly,
                I think ;
Let's plunge into Folly
                And sink !

Turn on the gramophone, boys!
I'm rapidly losing my poise;
   Try to avoid
   The subject of FREUD,
And let's make a horrible noise!

I will be Bohemian, I swear!
I don't care a hang what I wear;
   I'll take off my shoes
   And dance in the mews
Till I meet a policeman—so there!

I do like this party,
   I do!
But I don't feel so hearty—
   Do you?

I think I am going to yawn;
I've eaten too much of that brawn;
 I should have said
 We were better in bed,
And I strongly object to the dawn.

   I will be Bohemian, I swear!
   But I should like a little fresh air;
    I would not presume
    To suggest there's a gloom,
   But are we as gay as we were?

POOR MR. DAVENPORT

I'VE lost my job, George.
    It's—a—shame!
I've lost my job, George;
    All—the—same
I don't much care
    If I never see again
That Mrs. Davenport,
    She gives me a pain.

Well, there was I a-polishing
    The rods on the stairs—
Up comes the creature,
    And up she flares;
She lost her temper,
    And I give warning,
All about *nothing*, George!
    Oh, well, who cares?
But poor Mr. Davenport!
    Lord, how he'll miss me
    Now he can't kiss me
        Every morning
            On the stairs!

Well, there we are, George!
    Burned—my—boats.
Jealousy's a thing, George,
    Gets—girls'—goats.
Would you believe it?
    The mean old tabby
Took my notice,
    An' it do seem shabby.
Well, what's a kiss, George?
    I can't see the harm.
What can you expect
    When a girl's got charm?
But bang goes my income!
    We can't get married, George,
Not for a long time—
    George, will you mind?

And poor Mr. Davenport!
    Lord, how he'll miss me,
    Now he can't kiss me—
        And he *was* so kind!

ONE OF THE BEST

I THINK I've done with Mabel Grey,
A perfect woman in her way;
With Mabel one can never say,
  But I believe I'm jilted.
I met her first on Folkestone pier,
The night was very far from clear,
And absent-mindedly, I fear,
  I wooed her, and she wilted;
Well, you'd have done the same that night,
The moon was very weird and white,
And had it been electric light
  Perhaps I'd not have tarried;

But Mabel is the sort that makes
The most of gentlemen's mistakes,
And then one day a fellow wakes
　　And finds that he is married.

Dear old Mabel—one of the best!
　　But no more Mabel for me!
　Dogged, athletic, and strong as the sea
　　(And goodness, how strong a strong woman can be!)
Blessings on Mabel, and many times blest
　　Be the man who has stolen my Mabel from me!

I never had a fault to find
With Mabel; she was clean and kind,
But still she would improve my mind
　　And take me off to chapels;
She interfered with people's sins,
She'd set her heart on having twins,

She made me live on vitamins
　　And start the day with apples;
And so I told the constant hen
I could not marry her just then,
She said it did not matter when,
　　For she was used to waiting;
Nor did it matter where I went,
She patiently pursued the scent,
And took the fastest train, intent
　　On ultimately mating.

Dear old Mabel—one of the best!
 But no more Mabel—Hooray!
 Talk about goodness, she was good to me
 (And goodness, how good a good woman can be!)
Blessings on Mabel, and who would have guessed
  That somebody'd steal my sweet Mabel away?

I said, " Sweet Mabel, you're a saint,
But if you think I am, I ain't;
I ought to tell you that I paint
    Young ladies in their undies;

I love the bottle, I confess,
My morals are a horrid mess,
And Brighton is my one address
    On Saturdays and Sundays."

I said, "I doubt if we should suit,
I am a most disgusting brute."
She did not seem to care a hoot,
    But told me in a letter
It long had been her girlish plan
To marry some abandoned man
And mould him as a woman can—
    The worse I was the better.

Dear old Mabel—one of the best!
    But no more Mabel for me!
   A slave to hay-fever, but straight as a tree
   (And goodness, how straight a straight woman
      can be!)
Mabel be blest, and an annual rest
    To the man who has taken my Mabel from me!

And so I took a nobler line,
Behaving very pure and fine:
I gave up coffee, sweets, and wine,
    And let old ladies bore me;

And lo! the better I became
The lower burnt my Mabel's flame,
The less that Mabel saw to blame,
    The less did she adore me.
Instead, I think, she does adore
A very bad solicitor
Who likes his liquor more and more
    And never goes to chapels.
At any rate, she has a plan
To marry and reform the man
As only a good woman can—
    They say he's eating apples.

So here's to Mabel—barrels and bins—
    For it's no more Mabel for me!
  Earnest, intelligent, masculine she
  (And goodness, how male a male woman can be!)
Blessings on Mabel, and apples and twins
    To the man who has stolen my Mabel from me!

THE PEACH ON THE PILLION

RIDE on, pretty Percy!   I'm clinging, I'm clinging!
    I've needles and pins
    From my skull to my shins,
There's dust in my eyes, but I'm singing, I'm singing,
  I'm Helen, or someone, and you are my knight.
    You've a peach on the pillion,
    A girl in a million,
      I'm clinging, I'm singing,
        And Brighton's in sight!

Ride on, my brave Percy ! I'm aching, I'm breaking,
    I haven't a bone
    That feels quite like my own,
I've broke a suspender, my stocking is shocking—

  I wonder just what that old gentleman said ?
    My HECTOR, my hero,
    My Notting Hill NERO,
      I'm lashed to the saddle,
        And Brighton's ahead !

Ride on, rapid Percy! Go faster, go faster!
Look round—do you mind?—
To make sure I'm behind,
But quicker! the quicker, the sicker the Vicar,
He's waving, he's raving, the funny old dear!
Your face is vermilion,
But I'm on the pillion,
I'm clinging, I'm singing,
And Brighton is near!

WHAT'S THE GAME?

YES, it's my birthday. And it's not the first
  I've sat and wished that someone would explain
Why I was born and nourished up and nursed
  Instead of dropped down some convenient drain.
Well, no one wants me, though a lot have tried,
  My luck is out, my reputation's torn;
Nobody'd care a button if I died,
  Yet what a fuss there was when I was born!

> *I was a beautiful baby,*
>   *And everyone crowded to see,*
> *For everyone swore that no baby before*
>   *Had been quite such a baby as me.*

273

But now I'm not wanted no more
Unless it's for scrubbing a floor,
And if that's what a person is for—
Well, what's the Big Idea?

I done my part in this depressing scene
  And never grudged a drop of elbow-grease,
I've scrubbed my steps and left my dishes clean

  And reckon I'm as good as the police;
And when some beetle throws his weight about
  I answers back with pardonable scorn:
"All right," I says, "my glamour's gone, no doubt,
  But you should have seen the fuss when I was born!"

I was a beautiful baby,
   The wonder of Paradise Row,
I was a lamb in my little blue pram
   As I rode about sucking my toe.
The neighbours would stand in a queue
  To hold me a minute or two—
  But now I'm a blot on the view—
   Well, what's the Big Idea?

I must have been a little beauty then.
  Still, what did my poor mother want with me?
Well, I was number nine—or was it ten?—
  So Father took her purse and went to sea,
And Uncle knocked him down and went to jail,
  And Father died of jaundice off Cape Horn,
And Grandpa popped it when he heard the tale—
  O dear, there was a fuss when I was born!

> *I was a wonderful baby,*
>   *And the prettiest bud on the bough,*
> *I'd only to speak, and they'd laugh for a week,*
>   *But no one don't laugh at me now.*
>   *But if no one don't want me no more,*
>   *What for was I wanted before?*
>   *Well, what I mean, what am I for?*
>   *Oy! What's the game?*

THE SURPRISING SONG OF THE KING'S
COUNSEL

Now, Mrs. Green, attend to me,
For I'm Sir Buster Blow, K.C.
    The question what
    Is true or not
        Is highly complicated,
And while I would not say that you
Have stated that which is not true,

It is my case
That what took place
    Was not as you have stated.
Not that it matters, Ma'am, a lot
If what you've said was true or not,
    For I've a knack
    Of making black
    Resemble white or yellow,
And in ten minutes, Ma'am, or less,
The Judge, the Jury and the Press
    Will all decide
    That you have lied
    And I'm a clever fellow!

Blow! Blow! Sir Buster Blow!
Sir Buster Blow's a-blowing!

Nor hope with nimble repartee
To get the better, Ma'am, of me;

10*

No woman yet
Contrived to get
  Away with that, young lady!
Though I may call you any name
Don't think that you can do the same,
 For I'm afraid
 You are not paid
  To show that I am shady.
But I have been retained to blast
Your future and expose your past,
 A process which
 Will make you itch
  But move the Court to chuckles!
And if you falter, blush or blink,
The Jury will know what to think,
 While if you try
 A smart reply,
  The Judge will rap your knuckles.

Blow! Blow! Sir Buster Blow!
Sir Buster Blow's a-blowing!

Now take your mind back, Mrs. Green.
Where were you, please, at 8.15
    On Saturday
    The 6th of May?
        And were you wearing knickers?
And did you, Mrs. Green, or not
Spend Easter Monday in a yacht?

And do you swear
The persons there
    Consumed teetotal liquors?
Would it be Friday then, or June?
Who else went up in the balloon?
    Why did he fall?
    You can't recall?
        Well, that will suit me nicely.

You knew Lord Lavender, I think,
Who died not long ago of drink?
    You've never read
    A book in bed?
       I thought as much.   Precisely!

Blow! Blow! Sir Buster Blow!
Sir Buster Blow's a-blowing!

Now at the age of one or two
Were you discovered at the Zoo,
    Abandoned in
    A biscuit-tin
        By your ungrateful mother?

At any rate—I see you wince—
You have not seen your parents since,
    But after that
    Were nourished at
        Some nunnery or other?
Have you a mole behind the ear?
Do you prefer thick soup or clear?
    And when you dine
    Do you take wine,
        Dear Mrs. Green, or water?
I thought as much! I knew the face.
My Lord, I must conclude the case—

Embrace me, dear!
My Lord, it's clear
    The witness is my daughter!

Blow! Blow! Sir Buster Blow!
   Sir Buster Blow's a-blowing!

STORIES

In the café or the club,
At the Palace or the pub,
You are sure to meet a genial soul
Who apparently devotes
All the day to anecdotes
And has very little self-control.

283

In a minute you'll have heard
About the Bishop and the Bird,

And the liner, and the Lord-knows-who,
    And in very little more
    You'll be thinking " What a bore !
I shall have to tell a story too."
    But I never can recall
    Any anecdote at all,
Whether drawing-room or otherwise,
    So when anyone begins
    " Have you heard about the twins . . .?"
I delicately thus replies :

    " Everybody tells me stories,
        But I never know any stories,
            So don't you tell me a story,
                For I can't tell you a story,

I don't want to tell you a story,
  You don't want me to tell you a story,
    So if you don't tell me a story
      Then everything is quite all right."

Nothing daunted, he proceeds
To enumerate the deeds
Of a gentleman who owns a Ford,
  And continues with a short
  But scandalous report
Of a very very well-known lord;

While I wonder in despair
What the witticisms were
That were whispered in my ear last night—
  That extremely funny yarn
  Of the Banker and the Barn?
I remember little bits, not quite.
  But at any rate I'll miss
  Not a syllable of this,
And I listen as the children do

Am I feeble in the head?
By the time I go to bed
I have quite forgotten that one too.

Everybody tells me stories,
But I don't know any stories,
I don't want to hear good stories,
For I can't remember good stories!
I don't want you to tell me a story,
For I can't tell you a story,
But if you don't tell me a story,
Then everything is quite all right.

How I wish I had a brain
That was able to retain
All the captivating things one hears!
How I wonder who invents
All the spicy incidents
That are common in the lives of peers!
How I envy all the men
Who have heard about the hen
And can tell you how the Scotchman dined—
Though I very often tries
To pretend that I despise
This extraordinary kind of mind.
For you'll find that when a bloke
Always knows the latest joke
There is very little else he knows.
So I'd rather give the time
To the Cult of the Sublime,
And whenever he arrives I goes!

Everybody tells me stories,
  But I never know any stories.
   I'll shoot if you tell me a story,
     For I'll have to tell you a story,
      And I can't tell you a story,
         And I don't want to tell you a story!
            But if you don't tell me a story,
               Then everything is quite all right.

COALS OF FIRE

" WELL, Mrs. Rogers,
 I hear you're taking lodgers—
And young enough, they say, to be your son,

Now Rogers is away, dear,
    You're moping, I daresay, dear,
And company is pleasant if it's only just the one.

* "No offence took,*
*   I trust, where none intended?*
*   Don't leap before you look;*
*   Least said, the soonest mended.*
And as to what the gentleman is paying,
* Don't think it's any interest for me,*
Still, I thought you'd like to know what some was saying,
* So I though I'd tell you what was said, you see."*

"Thank you, Mrs. Bubble,
    But spare yourself the trouble;
I'm sure it's very good of you to call,
    And you not very well, dear,
    It's difficult to tell, dear,
But are you quite the same since you had that
    nasty fall?

* "No offence took,*
*   I trust, where none intended?*
*   Don't leap before you look;*
*   Least said, the soonest mended.*
But Alice said that you'd been hearing double
* Since Bubble threw that hammer at your head;*
Of course, I know she's very thick with Bubble,
* But still, I thought I'd tell you what was said."*

" Thank you, Mrs. Rogers,
    But, speaking of the lodgers,
Do you mean to have another, dear, or not ?
        That's what I should do, dear.
        He'll be lonely, just with you, dear ;
Though I'm sure it's very cosy with those nice new
    blinds you've got.

        " No offence took,
    I trust, where none intended ?
        Don't leap before you look ;
    Least said, the soonest mended.
I'm sorry for the boy, and him in mourning,
    Though Mabel don't believe the wife is dead ;
That Mabel says too much, I give you warning,
    But still, I thought I'd tell you what she said."

" Thank you, Mrs. Bubble.
    Now how about your trouble ?
Is Bubble backing losers just the same ?
        You've lost a lot of hair, dear,
        You ought to take more care, dear ;
But there, he's dragged you down, dear—I don't
    say you're to blame.

        " No offence took,
    I trust, where none intended ?
        Don't leap before you look ;
    Least said, the soonest mended.

You'll have a cup of tea?   I've got it handy.
  I daresay it's a long time since your last.
Well, Mabel said you breakfasted on brandy,
  And I'd better tell you what remarks is passed."

MARY THE MINX

EVERYBODY thinks
That Mary is a minx
(Whatever a minx may be),
  She likes high jinks,
  Wears blues and pinks,
And many people winks at we;
  The young men tear
  Their silly hair,
They get no share in she, Sir,
  And I don't much mind
  If she minx man-kind,
For she isn't a minx to me, Sir!

Everybody thinks
That Mary is a minx,
And many people shrinks
From Mary.

But one man's minx is another man's mate,
And here and now I hotly state,
If Mary is a minx
I'll stand you drinks
If you know a better minx
Than Mary.

I have an Aunt
Who says I can't
This wild young plant control;
My Uncle moans
" I *like* Miss Jones,
But, boy, she owns

no soul."
Well, you can keep
Your dreamers deep,

Your solemn sheep and Sphinxes!
  There's not much wrong
  With a minx as long
As a man don't mix his minxes!

Everybody thinks
That Mary is a minx,
And the parson shrinks
    From Mary;
But half the Duchesses I know
Were minxes not so long ago,

And if Mary is a minx,
Then circulate the drinks
If you know a better minx
    Than Mary.

I CAN'T
COME OUT TO-NIGHT

18563 Euston? Yes, that's right.
        Is that you, Joe?
I'm sorry, Joe, I can't come out to-night.
        Hullo? Hullo?
    I can't come out, my dear,
    They've got a party here . . .
        Won't let me go . . .
        What's that? I know.
        Hullo? Hullo?
I told her you was sailing in the morning,
I tell you, Joe, I nearly give her warning . . .
But there it is—I thought I'd telephone . . .
You'll have to go to Lovers' Lane alone . . .
        Hullo? Hullo?
        I'm sorry, Joe.
    I can't come out to-night.

Well, I suppose that this must be Good-bye . . .
      It seems a shame . . .
I tell you, Joe, I've had a good old cry . . .

      But, all the same,
    She's in the right, no doubt,
    It's not my evening out
      (Three minutes more?
      Yes. Make it four).
        Hullo? Hullo?
Well, such is life. What must be, must, I say.
This time to-morrow you'll be far away.
I only hope you'll have a pleasant trip,
I'm glad there aren't no women on the ship . . .
        Hullo? Hullo?
        It's no good, Joe.
      I can't come out to-night.

Well, think of me, Joe, washing pans and such . . .
      Think of me, Joe.
Send me a wireless, if it's not too much . . .
      Hullo?   Hullo?
      And if you stop at Spain,
      Think all the girls are plain,

      And tell them straight
      You're keen on Kate . . .
         Hullo?   Hullo?
You will take care with them Australians, Joe?
They are a bad, designing lot, I know.

Write to me, Joe, and don't you tell me whoppers . . .
Three minutes more?   No, I've got no more
coppers . . .
Hullo?   Hullo?
Good-bye, my Joe.
God bless you, Joe.   Good-night.

DON'T LOOK AT US!

THE SONG OF THE SHRINKING CHORUS.

DEAR Ladies and Gentlemen, *don't* look at us!
We shrink from attention, we deprecate fuss.
We're paid to expose to the popular eye
Our faces and forms, and we have to comply.

   But we know we look sights
   In these heliotrope tights,
  And, apart from the tights, we are shy;
So, although we are waving our legs in the air,
You'll kindly oblige us by looking elsewhere.

   Don't look at us!
    We are so shy.
   Be generous,
    And hide your eye.
  Ignore, we beg, the shapely leg
   We coyly kick before us.
  We do it just because we must—
   We are the Shrinking Chorus.

300

We come from the Country, the daughters of Squires,
We'd love to be living like mice in the Shires,
And nothing but poverty, hard to endure,
Could have driven us into the limelight, be sure,

For, try as we may
To look naughty and gay,
In fact we're fatiguing and pure,
And the rose in our cheeks as towards you we rush,
Isn't paint, as you think, but a maidenly blush.

Don't look at us!
    And do not think
We're amorous
    Because we wink.
We don't want notes from giddy goats—
    In point of fact they bore us;
We cannot bear the manly stare—
    We are the Shrinking Chorus.

Young noblemen, do not believe all you hear!
It is *not* our ambition to marry a Peer.
So don't ask us out at the end of the show,
Our mothers are sitting up waiting, you know.
        An occasional present
        Of flowers is pleasant,
    But orchids *embarrass* us so.
Nor should we be plied with unsuitable liquors,
For two of our number are married to Vicars.

Don't look at us!
    Our labours done,
We catch the bus
    To Kensington.
We should be bored if any lord
    Attempted to adore us;
We are the girls who don't want pearls—
    We are the Shrinking Chorus.

THE LUCKY BABY

My father went off with a gipsy,
　　Had seventeen children and died;
My mother was touchy and tipsy,
　　But I was her joy and her pride;
And many's the penny I've brought her
　　Down Ascot and Newmarket way—
She'd hold up her seventeenth daughter
　　To the lords and the ladies, and say:

"*Spare a copper for the Lucky Baby,*
　　Lucky Elizabeth Maud!
305

She'll bring you such luck, sir,
You never have struck, sir,
Health, winners, and travel abroad.
Hold up, Lucky Liz, show his lordship your phiz—
How's that for a fortunate face?
The last and the luckiest,
Prettiest, pluckiest,
Lucky Elizabeth Grace!"

My face was my fortune, she told me,
   And that's all the fortune I've seen;
I loved a young man, but he sold me,
   And I married the next at eighteen.
Well, one thing leads on to another,
   My husband has left me again,
And now I'm a happy young mother,
   At Epsom you'll hear me complain:

" Throw out your coppers for the Lucky Baby,
   Lucky Elizabeth Loo!
      You couldn't refuse her,
      You won't have a loser—

Milord, you've a lucky face too.
Hold up, Lucky Rose, show the lady your nose;
Now ain't that a fortunate eye?
The first one is lucky,
They say, don't they, ducky?
God bless you, milady—good-bye!"

"Spare a copper for the Lucky Baby,
And blessings shall be your reward.
She's a regular fairy,
Brought luck to Queen Mary,
Health and wealth to the motherless lord.
Who sent the kind stork to the Duchess of York,
And cured our dear Prince of his pain?
Well, you ask the Prince
If he's had the croup since
He was good to Elizabeth Jane!"

SATURDAY NIGHT

IT'S Saturday night, and I'm feeling all reckless;
I'll stand you a cider, I'll buy you a necklace;
We'll go to the pictures and settle down snugly;
You be my MARY and I'll be your DOUGLY.

I feel so bright
On a Saturday night,
I want to jump over the moon;

I want to change hats
With a lady, and that's
A sign there'll be trouble quite soon.
Douggie, my boy!
Mary, ahoy!
Come to the pictures and register joy,
For it's jolly old Saturday,
Mad-as-a-Hatter-day,
Nothing-much-matter-day-night!

It's Saturday night, I could fight the whole town—
Just say the word and I'll knock a man down.
Monday won't happen again till next week;
You be my soul-mate and I'll be your Sheikh.

Saturday night!
Saturday night!
I'm a rash irresponsible spark;

11*

Let's get a box
Of the two-shilling chocs,
And gobble them up in the dark.
Soul-mate, hullo!
Sheikhy, what-ho!
Come to the pictures and let yourself go,
For it's jolly old Saturday,
Mad-as-a-Hatter-day,
Nothing-much-matter-day-night!

It's Saturday night and I like your new hat;
I'm ready to pop with emotion and that;
I'm fizzy and fiery and fruity and tense,
So let's have a sundae and hang the expense!

Saturday night!
Saturday night!
I want to make Hammersmith hum;

I'm longing to thump
A piano, or jump
Up and down on the top of a drum.
Harriet, Hi!
Light of my eye!
Come to the pictures and have a good cry,
For it's jolly old Saturday,
Mad-as-a-Hatter-day,
Nothing-much-matter-day-night!

ONE OF THE MUGS

LONG, long ago, we were taught by our mothers
There's two kinds of people, the Mugs and the Others;
And, since I was promoted from bottles to jugs,
I've known very well that I'm one of the mugs.

I'm one of the mugs. Are you?
I'm diddled whatever I do.
I'm a mug, I'm a mutt, I'm a bathead, a boob,
I buy all the things advertised in the Tube;
Put my shirt on a horse, it lies down on the course.
I'm one of the mugs. Are you?

It's seven to one if I meet with a stranger,
His little girl's ill and her life is in danger.
His purse has been stolen, his home is at Ryde,
And he's longing to to get to the little one's side.

Well, I'm one of the mugs, I know,
But trouble unmans me so;
He's sure to be wearing the old college tie,
So I float him a loan and I kiss him good-bye,
And then I sit down and I have a good cry.
I'm one of the mugs. Are you?

I long for some dashing affair of the heart,
But a dear little dog is my usual part;
I fetch her umbrella and carry her bag,
And my dear little tail has a permanent wag.

I'm one of the mugs, I am,
A poodle, a pet, and a lamb.

For seven long years I've been nice to her mother,
While over my shoulder she ogled another,
And now it turns out what she wants is a brother.
  I'm one of the mugs.   Are you?

I'm constantly spoiling a Treasury note
For those healthy tobaccos that cure a sort throat,
Those magical systems that double your wits,
And gargles and dopes for the nerves or the nits.

  I'm one of the mugs, you see;
    They're mainly invented for me.
If you want an infallible thing for the hair,
Just look in the bathroom—they're all of them there,

But you'll notice my innocent belfry is bare.
I'm one of the mugs. Are you?

I'm much in request with old ladies and vicars;
I'm seen a mile off by the confidence-trickers,
And though my finances may leak like a sieve,
It's a comfort to think of the pleasure I give.

I'm one of the mugs, you see,
They're all of them looking for me.
The bookmaker's children are crying for bread,
And they murmur a Thank-you to me if they're fed.
But I wonder, I own—am I really alone?
I'm one of the mugs. Are you?

I CAN'T THINK WHAT HE SEES IN HER

JEALOUSY'S an awful thing and foreign to my nature;
I'd punish it by law if I was in the Legislature.
One can't have all of anyone, and wanting it is mean,
But still, there is a limit, and I speak of Miss Duveen.

I'm not a jealous woman,
But I can't see what he sees in her,
I can't see what he sees in her,
I can't see what he sees in her!
If she was something striking
I could understand the liking,
And I wouldn't have a word to say to that;
But I can't see why he's fond
Of that objectionable blonde—
That fluffy little, stuffy little, flashy little, trashy little,
creepy-crawly, music-hally, horrid little CAT!

I wouldn't say a word against the girl—be sure of
that;
It's not the creature's fault she has the manners of
a rat.
Her dresses may be dowdy, but her hair is always
new,
And if she squints a little bit—well, many people do.

I'm not a jealous woman,
 But I can't *see what he sees in her,*
  I can't *see* what *he sees in her,*
   I can't see what he sees *in her!*
He's absolutely free—
There's no bitterness in me,
Though an ordinary woman would explode;
 I'd only like to know
 What he sees in such a crow
As that insinuating, calculating, irritating, titivating,
 sleepy little, creepy little, sticky little TOAD !

COME TO BRITAIN

Oh, why does New York go to France for its fun
When they might be as jolly in South Kensington?
Why flock to the Continent? Surely they know
We've got a whole Continent parked in Soho.

Come to Britain! for Britain's the best.
It's eleven o'clock, and the nation's at rest.
The curfew is pealing, all's quiet at Ealing,
And no one can say we're offensively gay;
An income-tax form is the only thing cheap,
But come to Britain and have a good sleep.

319

Why go to Paris, you travelling swells,
When you've never had fun in our country hotels?
There isn't a bath, and the bell doesn't ring,
But you don't come to Britain for that sort of thing.

Come to Britain! The rooms are so old
And so picturesque that you won't mind the cold.
The bed's over there

and the light's over here;
Don't put out your boots if you want them this year;
The maid has a beard, the cold mutton perspires,
But come to Britain and visit the Shires!

Some of you find that Mentone is dull—
Come over and try a wet Sunday in Hull.
Take luncheon in bed, and get up when you dine,
But order your hot-water bottle for nine.

Come to Britain and lead the gay life!
As a rule it's illegal to bathe with your wife;

We censor all dramas that mention pyjamas,
But still there's a thrill in our girl-guides at drill;

Then we've swings in the parks, and municipal boats,
So come to Britain and sow your wild oats!

Come to Britain!   We've done what we could
To make the place healthy and wholesome and good.
Your whisky will cost you much less in the States,
And here, between drinks, we have tedious waits,
But the Albert Memorial's always on show,
So come to Britain, and let yourselves go!

DON'T BE A TEETOTALLER, DADDY!

Don't be a teetotaller, Daddy!
  It never did no one no good.
It'll make you all funny and faddy,
  And Mother would hate it, she would.
What happened to Bill when he gave up the beer?
  It was Providence working, no doubt—
He rowed on the Thames and was washed down a weir—
  I'd rather you knocked us about.

Don't you take up with any treatment, Dad.
You're awful, drunk, but sober you're as bad.

And now we do know what we've got to nurse,
But, stop the drink, it might be something worse.
These temperance-folk have all got horrid vices,
With some it's chocolates, with others ices;
I'd sooner see you reeling down the streets
Than sit like Mr. Lizard, sucking *sweets!*

Don't be a teetotaller, Daddy!
Once start, it's a puzzle to stop.
You'd only go funny and faddy,
And work overtime at the shop.
Remember how Bert threw his whisky away,
And lived on Imperial fruits?
He's a slave to his hot-water-bottle to-day—
I'd rather you slept in your boots.

Say what you like, there's this about the drink,
It makes you talk, instead of only think,
And anything that helps the conversation
Is beneficial to the British nation.
And these teetotallers have dreadful habits—
That Mr. Mole has give his life to *rabbits!*

I'd sooner see you have your little bouts
Than keep white mice or organise the Scouts.

Don't be a teetotaller, Daddy!
You'll never be cheerful no more.
You'll only go funny and faddy,
And give all you've got to the pore.
What happened to Henry, who took the good path,
And joined a No-Alcohol Club?
He reads in his bed and he sings in his bath—
We'd rather you went to the pub.

TRIANGULAR LEGS

I SHOULD not presume to express any view
    On the Modernist Movement in Art,
But I've studied the work of Elizabeth Glue,
    And this I can say from the heart—
        She can do what she please
        With her houses and trees
    And I shall not attempt to advise,
        But I do not believe
        That the daughters of Eve
Have such *very* triangular thighs.

No doubt there are women with indigo necks
    And heliotrope hips to be found,
But I should have said that the shape of the sex
    Was not so much oblong as round;
        Paint peonies green
        And I see what you mean,
    Paint eyes like an ostrich's eggs,
        But *is* it the case
        That the girls of our race
Have such *very* triangular legs?

I do not know much of the feminine tribe,
    But I've watched one or two in the Tube,
And I've seen very few you could fairly describe
    As a couple of squares and a cube;
        But that is the view
        Of Elizabeth Glue,
    And my vision with sympathy swims
        When I think of the boobs
        Who are married to cubes
With a set of triangular limbs.

Was Sheba the Queen, who made Solomon gape,
  A collection of parallel lines?

Was Juliet just an elliptical shape
  With a few geometrical signs?

Elizabeth Glue,
Give me anything new,
And I'll swallow it down to the dregs,
But *did* Helen of Troy
Run away with the boy
On such *very* triangular legs?

PLAIN JANE; OR, THE BREAD-WINNER

A Tragedy for Music.

The table set for breakfast. Seated at the table are Miss Jane Surbiton *and the* Rev. Frederick Tate, *agitated.*

Jane. Will you take coffee, Mr. Tate—or tea?

The Rev. Tate. Coffee. Or tea. Or may I have
    the two?
  Well, no, say tea. Say coffee. Well, you see,
  I don't want either. All I need is you.

(Falling on his knees—first one and then the other.)

        Jane! Jane!
        Beautiful Jane!
      Others may call you plain,
  But beauty is hidden in curious shapes;
  People have found some attraction in apes;
  Some love the lily and some like the leaf,
  Some adore mutton and some prefer beef;
  Brighton is beautiful, seen from the sea,
  But you from all angles are lovely to me,
       My Jane! Jane!
  Beautiful, beautiful, beautiful, beautiful Jane!
             (They embrace.)

Enter WINNIE, MRS SURBITON.

JANE. Dearest Mamma, we are to be united!

MRS. SURBITON. What—before breakfast? Well, I
    am delighted!

JANE. It's splendid, is it not? But we would rather
    That it was you who broke the news to father.

MRS. SURBITON. Your father, child, though he is
    good and kind,
    Is not his best at breakfast, I allow.

JANE. That's very true. But Fred may change his
    mind.
    Waste not a moment, Ma. Tell father *now*.
        (*A bellowing, off.*)

MR. GEORGE SURBITON *comes in dressed for the City,
    but in bedroom slippers, and singing fiercely
    a stanza from the celebrated hymn to "Bacon
    and Eggs," in which all join, seated.*

"O breakfast, O breakfast, the meal of my heart!
  Bring porridge, bring sausage, bring fish for a start,
  Bring kidneys and mushrooms and partridges' legs,
  But let the foundation be bacon and eggs.
      Bacon and eggs,
      Bacon and eggs,
        Bring bacon,
        Red bacon,
      And let there be eggs!"

    (*Meanwhile* MR. SURBITON *picks up "The
    Times," studies it with ill-concealed con-
    cern, and, after several explosive snorts,
    indicates his opinion of the State of Things.*)

Well, I wonder more and more
What the Government is for!
England's going to the dogs,
Both my eggs are cold as frogs,
Things are very, very queer;
Kindly take this down, my dear.

(*He dictates, eating, and* MRS. SURBITON *takes
down the following letter to "The Times."*)

To the Editor of " The Times."

SIR, I crave a tiny fraction
  Of your valuable space
To record my stupefaction
  At the follies of the race.
While the Young with harmful pleasures
  Rush regardless to the tomb,
Parliament with mad-cap measures
  Hurries on our country's doom.
Frankly, Sir, my view is fervent,
  Something must at once be done.
I am, your obedient Servant,
  GEORGE ISAIAH SURBITON.

ALL (*with every sign of sympathetic approval*).
    What an admirable letter!
JANE. After that he'll feel much better.
MRS. SURBITON. Do you feel better, dear?
MR. SURBITON.   I do.
MRS. SURBITON. Then I should like a word with you.

(*She lays a fond caress on* MR. SURBITON'S
*head, who receives it with no extravagant
enthusiasm.*)

MRS. SURBITON (*wounded*). Have you forgot, my pet,
   What day it is to-day?
  It is the day we met,
   It is the fifth of May;
  It is the day we met,
   You kissed me on the pier;
  I wore my Whitby jet,
   You had hay-fever, dear.
  Ah, say I'm not mistaken—
   You feel the old, old thrill?
  Turn from your eggs and bacon
   And say you love me still.

MR. SURBITON (*shortly*). Quite true.
        I do.

(*Aside*) Cursed is the wife who is not able
  To curb her passions at the table,
  But breakfasts like a billing dove
  And mixes marmalade with love!
  Will they not learn, have they not read,
  Man cannot love till he has fed?
  (*He returns to the Financial Column and his
   wife to the charge.*)

MRS. SURBITON. And now our daughter Jane,
   Sweet replica of you
  (She has her father's brain,
   She has hay-fever too),
  Has on the self-same date
   That sealed her father's fate
  Selected for her mate
   The Reverend Frederick Tate.
  Oh, by the recollection
   Of twenty years ago,

On their demure affection
Your blessing, George, bestow !
(*But Mr. Surbiton is lost in the Financial Column.*)
MR. SURBITON. " Rice was steady, Lead was easy.
Tin was not in much request,
Jute was feeble, Wool was wheezy,
Copper never looked its best."
And it is just as well, I think,
That all my money is in Zinc——
Coffee, my love ?
MRS. SURBITON(*wounded still worse—indeed in anger*).
For twenty years you've trampled me past bearing,
For twenty years not noticed what I say,
For twenty years not seen what I was wearing,
For twenty years forgot my wedding-day——
MR. SURBITON (*passing up his cup, absently*).
Coffee, my dear ? It is an odd reflection,
In all the changes of our common lot,
In twenty years of conjugal affection
I never yet have had my coffee hot.
(*He returns to " The Times." She weeps
quietly into the coffee.*)
FREDERICK (*in two minds, as usual*).
Well, if this is married life,
Is it wise to take a wife ?
Can it be that by degrees
Jane and I will grow like these ?
Will she while I break my fast
Lovingly recall the past,
Or, with ill-timed tenderness,
Irritate me while I dress ?
Will the flame which now I feel

        Dwindle at the morning meal?
        Could her kisses ever be
        Less to me than kedgeree?

JANE (*stopping the rot, removes him from the table and embraces him*). Kiss me, my love, and let them see
        How like some pink anemone
        My faithful rock, I cling to thee
          For all the world to view.
        So never shall this firm embrace
        My father's horrid hand unlace,
        For he that moves me from my place
          Must tear my heart in two.

MRS. SURBITON. Be careful, Jane, for in your conversation,
        Much as I sympathise with what you said,
      I note a strain of grim determination
        Which won't appeal to anyone you wed.

FREDERICK (*nervous*). Angelic Jane, have you forgot
        Your dear old father's on the spot?
        He has the cash, and we have not,
          And that's a point of view.
        Though money has no charms for me,
        And Love is more than £ *s. d.*,
        What I possess would, frankly, be
          Inadequate for two.

JANE (*kneels at* MR. SURBITON'S *knee, which he hates —still nervouser*). Listen, listen, father dear,
        Before it be too late.
      For many a weary, weary year
          Your little Jane,
          Your plain, sweet Jane,
         Has hunted for a mate.

O'er hill and dale the slippery male
   I vainly have pursued,
With flattering tongue allured the young,
   The older ones with food.
And now that I have caught a man
Oh, let us keep him if we can!
    He's in the net,
    But even yet
     May wriggle through,
So, if you can in any way
Suggest that marriages are gay,
    And help me dish
    This timid fish,
     Dear father, do.

JANE, *her* MOTHER, *and* FREDERICK (*all kneeling,
but* FREDERICK *not so heartily*).

Breadwinner, Master of our Fates,
Householder, Payer of the Rates,
Approve these nuptials if you can,
And think yourself a happy man,
Who with a whisper can bestow
The highest bliss that mortals know.

(*They hang upon his words.* MR. SURBITON
*is almost moved, but unhappily his eye
wanders back to the Financial Column,
and he explodes.*)

MR. SURBITON (*waving " The Times " in a frenzy*).
Dogs and devils! what d'you think?
The bottom's dropping out of Zinc!
    Zinc is falling,
    Zinc's appalling,

> Zinc is in a dreadful state;
> > Zinc is crumbling,
> > Zinc is tumbling,
> Zinc is down to twenty-eight!
> I think we'll sink with zinc, my dove—
> Is this a time to talk of *love?*
> > Give me my boots!
> > Where are my boots?
> > Give me my *boots!*
> > Where are my BOOTS?
> > > All is up!
> > > The taxi toots—
> > > One more cup!
> > > The engine hoots,
> > > All is up!
> > > The beasts, the brutes!
> > > One more cup!
> > > Where are my BOOTS?

ALL. All is up, etc.

> (*Full orchestral agitato, while* MRS. SURBITON
> *prepares coffee and her daughter hunts
> boots.*)

THE REV. TATE (*philosophises apart*).
> Well, if this is married life,
> Man is mad to take a wife!
> Also, it occurs to me,
> What about heredity?
> These two parents, I confess,
> Magnetise me less and less;
> Am I then to plight my troth
> With one that has the faults of both?

Money was their only merit,
This, it seems, she won't inherit.
Fare you well, my dearest Jane,
We must never meet again.
I'll think of you—so do not cry—
But as a sister, Jane. Good-bye.

[MR. SURBITON, *booted at last, rushes from
the house with* FREDERICK, *both pausing
at the door to sing* Farewell! *In this
splendid chord the women join. They are
then left weeping, and quite right too.*

CURTAIN.

TWO GENTLEMEN OF SOHO

(It now appears that Shakespeare is best when played in modern clothes. Perhaps the themes of modern life would be better dressed in Shakespearean costume. Some may think this play wordy, but then there are brutes who think Shakespeare wordy. There is an acting version, shorter certainly, but much less beautiful.)

CHARACTERS:

THE DUCHESS OF CANTERBURY.
LADY LÆTITIA (*her daughter*).
HUBERT (*her dancing partner*).
LORD WITHERS.
TOPSY.
SNEAK (*a private detective*).
PLUM (*a public detective*).
A WAITER.

SCENE.—*A Night-Club. Three tables. The middle table empty.* TOPSY *reading a book at Table One.* PLUM, *suspicious, at Table Three. Music in the ballroom, off.*

PLUM. Ho, girl, look up! A goblet of champagne?
TOPSY. I thank you, no. Indeed, 'tis after hours.

(Returns to book.)

PLUM *(downcast, aside).*

I am an officer from Scotland Yard,
Dressed in the likeness of an English lord,
And night by night, while seven weeks swung by,
Have I to this lewd haunt made pilgrimage
In search of some irregularity,
Cheating an entrance with a lusty lie
(But all's forgiven in a noble cause),
Sometimes disguisèd as a gentleman,
And sometimes in the costume of a virgin.

But nothing happens. I have offered bribes,
I have been suppliant for sweet wine or opium
After the hours by Parliament provided,

But like the fabulous Mongolian drop
Of water on strong rock for ever falling,
I have made no impression.   I believe
There is no falsehood practised here but mine,
There is no jot nor tittle of the law
By these respectable impostors broken.
Well, this is hard.   Only the dear old Duchess
Has with my bitterness some sweet compounded
Of nimble dances and beguiling looks,
But she engagèd with Another is.
So, gentle Sleep, upon my eyelids press,
And let me wake to catch some wickedness.

(Sleeps—Music.)

Enter LADY LÆTITIA *and* LORD WITHERS.   *They
sit at Table Two.*

LÆTITIA.   What is this place?
WITHERS.   My dear Lætitia,

I do misdoubt I do it too much honour,
And you too little, by this introduction.
It is a night-club. You have seen a stone
Turned by a ploughman on the hills of Kent,
And the foul creeping many-legged things
Which dart from under, blinking in the light?
So from this den snatch suddenly the lid
Between the midnight and the milkman's hour,
You will see slink and scutter about Soho
The very dregs and sediment of London:
Here the hot cits of Wimbledon and Streatham
With busy rakes from Kensington combine
In obscene alchemy to make the night
One long invention in debauchery,
Wine, women, drugs——

LÆTITIA.   In that case, Algernon,
Pardon my *ab*surd curiosity,
But what is't brings you to this hell-hole?

WITHERS.   Well,
I am a writer, and as some physician,
Searching the secrets of the human body,
Doth not the healthy but the sick pursue,
And is more happy 'midst unique distempers,
Growths, fevers, tumours, abscesses and boils,
Than with the strong and undefilèd flesh,
So in the study of these diseasèd minds
Do I seek knowledge not to be explorèd
In the dull wits of the respectable,
Sucking a sweetness from the poisoned flower,
And like the wombat savouring the cheese
When 'tis corrupted——

LÆTITIA.   Well, I cannot say
That I see any signs of dissipation.

WITHERS (*indicates* TOPSY *and* PLUM).

Mark then this lout, which in a rustic stupor
Is dead till morning, when it swills again.
Mark too this maiden that with Vestal eye
Seems to see nothing but the book she reads not—
Here's what they call a woman of the half-world,
That is, she is not one thing nor the other,
Dubs herself " dancing partner," and for hire
She will with any pursy sot that offers
Waltz, fox-trot, Charleston—the whole catalogue
Of modern antics—and the evening through,
Will counterfeit with some strange stockbroker
A mercenary satisfaction.   Pah!

(*Observes dancers, off.*)

And yet some follies may adorn the young
Which to the old must be disfigurement.
How yonder matron wallows in the dance,

A loaded waggon creaking down the hill
Of years and adiposity! The traffic
Bounds and rebounds unheeded from her flanks,
Or, pausing careless in her path, is crushed.
And on her breast is like a pendant hung
A slim, fair, pallid and perspiring youth
That smiles and smiles and smiles, and is in
   torture.
How like a milit'ry balloon she looks
That is entangled in an aspen-tree!
Do you not think so, dear?

LÆTITIA.   That is my mother.

WITHERS. Is't so? So 'tis!

LÆTITIA.   And that *her* dancing partner!

WITHERS. I never saw her here before, Lætitia!
These hands should quicker have torn out these
   eyes
Than these harsh lips have spoken, or these legs
Have carried me to these conclu-si-ons!

LÆTITIA. It is not easy to avoid Mamma,
On summer evenings she is everywhere.
There is no saxophone doth not salute her
· With other mothers rounder than herself,
Like baby elephants that after twilight
Jump in the jungle.

WITHERS.   'Tis the Age of Age.

LÆTITIA. How true! Age will be served, and this
   pale youth
Must for a salary (how much I know not)
The nightly partner of her gambols be.
O me, 'tis pitiful to see one's mother
Go to the dogs!

WITHERS. Weep not, Lætitia,
But let us have a dry Martini. Ho!

Enter a WAITER. PLUM *wakes up.*

PLUM. This is a Viscount, and I never saw
A lord that did not love to break the law.
(Watches.)

WITHERS. Pluck me ten berries from the juniper,
And in a beaker of strong barley-spirit
The kindly juices of the fruit compress.
This is our Alpha. Next clap on your wings,
Fly south for Italy, nor come you back
Till in the cup you have made prisoner
Two little thimblefuls of that sweet syrup
The Romans call Martini. Pause o'er Paris
And fill two eggshells with the French Vermouth.
Then home incontinent, and in one vessel
Cage your three captives, but in nice proportions,
So that no one is master, and the whole
Sweeter than France, but not so sweet as Italy.
Wring from an orange two bright tears, and shake,
Shake a long time the harmonious trinity,
Then in two cups like angels' ears present them,
And see there swims an olive in the bowl,
Which when the draught is finished shall remain
Like some sad emblem of a perished love.
This is our Omega. Go, fellow!
WAITER. Sir,
It is too late. I cannot serve you.
PLUM. Damn!
(Music; exit WAITER.)
WITHERS. O that in England might be born a Man,

Sprung from the loins of English liberty,
To rise and sweep, twice daily, like old Thames,
In a strong tide 'gainst petty tyrannies,
And though at evening he be beaten back
Flood in at morning to clean the channel again
Of busy women, and suck out to sea
Bans, prohibitions, interferences,
Movements, Societies, Government Departments,
Such as curtail, diminish, and cut down
The antique privilege of true-born Englishmen
To take their pleasure in what way they please,
When, how, which, where, whatever, and with
    whom!   (*Chord.*)
Was it for this I joined the Infantry
And took up arms against a Continent
To have my eating and my drinking times
Fixed by old maids and governed by policemen?
    [PLUM, *with dignity, passes out to ball-room.*
I think, were Germany the master here,
We should, at least, be certain of our beer.
    But see, the Duchess finds new company,
In age and form more fitter to her own!

LÆTITIA. It is the fellow who was here asleep.

WITHERS. Then I have wronged him, for the man is
    sober.

LÆTITIA. He would not else have undertaken Mother.

Enter HUBERT, *exhausted, and mopping brow. He
    sinks into chair beside* TOPSY, *who sits up and
    takes notice.*

WITHERS. And here, like some slim carrack long
    distressed
  In the rough storm and tempest of the ocean,

Comes the frail consort of her voyaging,
His sails awrack, his rigging in disorder,
And the proud pennant drooping at the peak!
Thankful he creeps into the nearest port,
Nor is there barge, punt, fishing-boat so humble
He will not gladly berth beside her.

TOPSY.   Sir,
You are distempered, and your breathing labours,
As I have seen some baby grampus pant
After a heavy supper. Why is this?

HUBERT. Oh, it were better to be bound with vipers
To the great stone of Sisyphus, and roll
All day for ever up and down the hill,
Than to be fastened to a human mountain
Aping the antics of an early lamb!
For one is punishment, pure, unmistaken,
But this—this is the sacrilege of Pleasure,
I do a treason to my youth, I am
Not Sisyphus, not Tantalus, but both!
It were enough to caper with a whale,
Or spin a waltz with a rhinoceros,
But to be jostled in the dance by fairies,
Young, unattainable, locked i' the arms
Of men not better but more blest than I am,
And on their soft and tantalising lips
See the slow smile that mocks my servitude—
This is my torture and damna-ti-on!

                                        (*Is overcome.*)

TOPSY. Be easy, Sir. This is my own employment.
I too must foot it and be gay for gold
With such as can get nobody for nothing.

HUBERT. Aye, but with many. I am bound to one.

TOPSY. Life is a most extraordinary thing.

HUBERT. Man, like a pebble on a glacier,
  Moves imperceptibly but always down.
TOPSY. Life is a looking-glass, in which we see
  Only the dull reflection of ourselves,
  And every day 'tis less attractive.
HUBERT.   Come,
  This is no time for dismal metaphor!
  My monster's busy—while I have the chance,
  Come, fellow-slave, console me in the dance!
          (*They get up, get out, and get off. Music.*)
WITHERS. I think between them there's a seed of love
  Which shall grow up into a goodly tree. (*Kneels.*)
  And you, Lætitia, so frosty-proud,
  Like to those castles of cold loveliness
  Which scare the shipping on the North Atlantic,
  So that old Captains sniff the sky and mutter:
  " There is an iceberg sixty miles away."
  Hushed are the passengers, and no more now
  The merry quoit rings lightly on the deck,
  But when the wonder bursts upon the view,
  Fear is forgotten—O Lætitia,
  You are so beautiful that I am bold,
  And dare defy the miracle with wooing.
  Will you not swim a moment in the sun
  Of my affection—from the Arctic waters
  Of dumb indifference drift southward soon,
  Hang in the middle latitudes, and then
  Melt into matrimony? Oh, I know
  'Tis not the mode to speak of marrying,
  And this warm sentiment which now inflames me
  Is but a mock and madness to the young.
  No more the sweet confusions of the simple,
  Rings, tokens, pledges, clutchings of the hands,

Partings and moons and memories are holy—
Nay, I have heard some yearling split his sides
At roses clustered round a cottage door
Or the fond statement of a negro's passion.
For now is devotion the stale jest of fools,
And that wild ecstasy the poets sang
Is but a livelihood and theme for doctors,
Policemen, clowns, and psycho-analysts,
While he that boldly on his knees professes
A fixed affection for a single person
Calls down the cackle of the continents.
Yet, though to speak these shameful syllables
Names me a Ninny, feeble in the mind,
In soul suburban—*Will you marry me?*

LÆTITIA. I am too much upset about my dam.
I think I shall not marry anyone,
But take my mother to a nunnery,
And there, with a little needlework, convert her
From the vain fancies of the world—but look!
I would not have her see me. Let us fetch
A circuit to the ball-room, and from there
Play spy to the event.

WITHERS.   It shall be so.

> [*They go off, right.*

Enter, left, the DUCHESS, *with* PLUM. *Fairy music.*

PLUM. I hope, Your Grace, I have not wearied you?

DUCHESS. There are the wings of swallows on your feet,
And in your arms the potency of lions.
It is not dancing when I dance with you,
I have no mind, no body, I am nothing
But a swift ghost that soars a prisoner
In the embraces of a flying bear.

PLUM. It is a pleasure to give satisfaction.

DUCHESS. Are you a member?

PLUM.   Duchess, I am not.

DUCHESS. Then with what member—nay, in this
     poor house
   What member moves with such a dignity,
   Hath such a grace and nimbleness of wit,
   That he dare vouch for such a visitor?

PLUM. I did not come with any, but alone.

DUCHESS. Is not a member, yet alone he came——
   Strange!

Enter SNEAK, *cloaked and masked. Chord.*

SNEAK (*darkly, apart*).
   So. She's here. And this gross gentleman
   Should be that paramour my daughter spoke of,
   The constant prop of ducal indiscretion.
   I will lie close and watch the giddy scene.
   Waiter!

WAITER.   What would you?

SNEAK.   I am a detective——
    Nay, do not tremble!—not His Majesty's,
    But the sworn servant of an Agency
    Skilled to pursue, see, tabulate, record,
    And in the courts most cunningly describe
    All the sly naughtiness of faithless wives,
    Or peccant husbands, as the case may be,
    Looks, nods, and greetings, holding-on of hands
    After the space by decency commanded,
    Meetings and partings, secret matinées,
    The sigh drawn upward or the blinds drawn down,
    Gifts, letters, notes—but are you listening?
WAITER. Ay.
SNEAK.   Well, His Grace the Duke of Canterbury
    Hath of our house requirèd information
    Touching the acts, deeds, conduct, and behaviour
    Of that loose elephant he calls his wife.
    Whether in truth he doth suspect her virtue,
    Whether the wish was father to the thought,
    And the old dog would find some cause for parting
    Such as himself he doth not dare to furnish,
    I cannot tell you.   But I do persever,
    Here is the reason, cause, and circumstance
    Why I sit here instead of somewhere else.
    And now that all lies naked as the noon
    In the hot deserts of Australia,
    Nor doth one leaf of artful stratagem,
    Lies, counterfeit, deception, subterfuge,
    Ingenious accent or oblique suggestion
    O'er the bare truth project one inch of shadow,
    And if there be a person here alive
    Who doth not now know better than his mother

My name, my calling, and my secret business,
Then it were better for the loon to be
Boiled in ammonia till his wits return——
Well, if all's clear, known, plain, and manifest,
Then there is nothing I would say but this,
What *I* should like would be a spot of whisky.

PLUM (*hearing, characteristically, last line only, pricks
    up ears*).   Now surely shall some misdemeanour
    follow !

DUCHESS. They say the antelope on summer nights
    Halts at the margin of the stream to drink.

PLUM. Fellow, we thirst ! Bring port and lemonade !

WAITER. God made the lemon and the grape together,
    But Man, milady, has divided them,
    And at this hour, by our wise Parliament,
    The lemon's lawful, but the grape's a crime.

DUCHESS (*unstrung*).
    What is this talk of Parliaments and lemons ?
    Am I a Duchess, to be fed on *lemons ?*
    Was there not somebody who *died* of lemons ?
    Did none arrest him nor none prosecute ?
    Is there no law against excessive lemons,
    Or too much sugar or intemperate tea,
    Or the vile craving for hot-water-bottles ?
    What !   Lemons ?   Parliaments ?   As I'm a
        Duchess,
    Bring me the article !

WAITER (*cowed*).   It shall be done.
    (*Takes bottle of port from pocket and places on table.*)

PLUM. Ho !   Bar the doors !   Sound the alarm
    without !   [*Exit* WAITER.
    Let none make entrance or emergencies !

Enter instantly LÆTITIA, LORD WITHERS, TOPSY,
and HUBERT.

WITHERS. What's here?
LÆTITIA.   How?
TOPSY.   So!
HUBERT.   What is't?
SNEAK.   Ha!
DUCHESS.   Who are you, sir?
PLUM. I am the Metropolitan Police,
  And this my warrant. Let a trumpet sound.
                                    (*Chord.*)

DUCHESS. O viper!
HUBERT.   Judas!
LÆTITIA.   Mother!
DUCHESS.   Oh, my daughter!   (*Sobs.*)
PLUM. Oh, it is anguish for a horse to suffer
  The opposing reins of office and affection
  Which right and left distract the tender mind!
  But this no Englishman has done, nor shall—

Make duty servant to his inclinations.
Take you these papers and at once write down
Your names and callings, titles, dignities,
Estates and mansions, orders, decorations,
Whether in wedlock you be joined or no,
How many children, houses, wives, convictions,
With all such details and appendages
As shall be pertinent.   And in the morning
At Bow Street presently make apparition.
Now to your homes go softly.

DUCHESS.   Oh, the shame!

HUBERT. I will not!

WITHERS.   Insolent!

LÆTITIA.   My mother!

SNEAK.   HOLD!

PLUM. Who's this that rudely doth resist the tide
    Of our proceedings?

SNEAK.   I am a detective,
    Now by the Duke of Canterbury charged
    To see, watch, notice, and at dawn discover
    The nightly conduct of this noblewoman——

DUCHESS. Now open, Earth, and hide me!

SNEAK.   " Sneak," said he,
    " Good, honest Sneak, if you have any skill
    Or any pity for a poor old man,
    Find me that snake and serpent in the grass
    Which hath drawn off my Duchess from her duty,
    So that in naughtiness and vain delights
    She doth dishonour the evening of our days
    And utterly neglects the housekeeping——
    Find me this worm, good Sneak, that I may split
      him!"

Thus the old Duke, with bloody fearful oaths,
Cleaning a pistol by his lonely bed,
Or whetting some great knife upon a stone;
And thus at daybreak shall I answer him.
" Duke, he is found, your ravisher of homes,
Snake in the grass and cuckoo in the nest,
A little, round, unpleasant, portly thing
Which crawls, part trespasser and part policeman,
Into the childish revels of the rich,
Toys with their wives and tramples on their toes,
Eats of their salt, and presently arrests them
For some sly spinster's quibble in the law,
And while he smiles contaminates the air
With artful ruse and mean suspi-ci-on,
Will call for wine to catch a flunkey out,
And drink with women only to denounce them——
This, Duke, is he that, doubly double-faced,
Hath the pure spirit of your wife corrupted,
Night after night entwinèd in the dance,
Which I with evidence can justify,
This scheming, slow, constabulary lump,
This is your libertine and co-respondent——"
PLUM (*enraged, takes truncheon from trousers*). Peace,
    caitiff !
SNEAK.   Ha !
PLUM.   Thou dog of Houndsditch !
DUCHESS.   Oh !
            (*They fight. Hurry Music.*)
SNEAK. What, bully ?
PLUM.   Sot !
SNEAK.   Hog !
PLUM.   Bastard !
DUCHESS.   Oh ! I swoon !

SNEAK. Ah, would you?

WITHERS.   Peace!

LÆTITIA.   O gentlemen!

PLUM.   Die, villain!

(SNEAK *dies.   Chord.*)

TOPSY (*prostrates self on body of* SNEAK).

   O Sir, you have killed my father!   Why was this?

   I had no life, no being, but in him,

   And now he's not I am not neither.   Oh!

(*Dies of grief.   Chord.*)

HUBERT (*kneels beside body of* TOPSY).

   O Topsy, Topsy, could you not have waited?
   I did not think that you would leave me thus,
   Without one word nor tender beckoning
   To bid me follow you. Yet I will follow,
   And make one date of all eternity.

                (*Strikes self on head with truncheon*
                     and dies.   Chord.)

PLUM. This was an issue not to be expected.

WITHERS. Yet I have heard some countryman re-
    mark,
   Clapping the swallows from a field of corn:
   " It is not seldom in the course of nature,
   After a drought, not in light showers only
   Falls and descends the gentle rain of Heaven,
   But in a spate and tempest——"

PLUM.   But what's here?

DUCHESS (*kneeling*).

   Now, Earth, receive me, for I die of shame!

WITHERS (*apart*). What does this bode?

LÆTITIA.   She spoke of death.

WITHERS. I heard her.

LÆTITIA. This must be hindered.

WITHERS. Ay.

PLUM. But mark what follows!

DUCHESS. Farewell to revelry, farewell the dance,
And the gay trappings of my second youth!
Farewell the music, and, sweet saxophone,
Thou art not music, yet I wish thee well,
With all late suppers and hot gala-nights,
The coloured streamer and the blue balloon,
Fans, rattles, dolls, and india-rubber dogs,
And wicked kippers eaten in the dawn,
And those fierce rhythmic and delicious tunes
Which light a fever in the veins and set
The feet, the soul, fermenting—fare you well!
   Oh, it is selfish in the Young to grudge us
The little joys of our declining days!
Have they not Love and Happiness their servants,
And must all Pleasure bow to them as well?
This were ungenerous. And I think in Heaven,
If there be saxophones as well as harps,
They are not only for the Young. But here
I shall not see a gala-night again.
                    (*Dies of shame. Fairy music.*)

LÆTITIA. Oh, she is dead!

WITHERS. Life, like a butterfly,
Hath from the window of this flesh departed.
I think I never did nor never shall
See any woman so impeccable.
She was a person of extreme distinction.
She had discretion, grace, nobility,
Beauty and strength, taste, wit, intelligence,

Was kind to animals, by children worshipped;
I think I never saw a woman——
LÆTITIA.   Peace!
Mother, shall any other lips but mine
Tell the long catalogue of your great virtues?
I was your child, and if in anything
From the straight furrow of the good you strayed,
I do accuse myself.   I should have told you
The snares and dangers of this wicked world,
And nursed you always with a daughter's love.
For you were too much guarded in your youth,

And knew not everything, as we know now,
Who by experience of all temptation
Against temptation are inoculated;
But you, poor innocent, were an easy prey;
The first shrill saxophone that squeaked in London
Was your undoing.   And where'er you be,
Whether 'tis harps or saxophones or timbrels
That now make mischief in your neighbourhood,

You shall not face that music quite alone.

> *(Dies of remorse.   Chord.)*

WITHERS. Thou, too, Lætitia, art thou dead?

PLUM.   She is.

WITHERS. Then there is no more virtue in the world,
Fire hath no heat, and the congealèd sun
Swims like a frozen orange in the sky,
There is not any meaning anywhere,
And to no purpose the great stars revolve!
Oh, my dear Tish, unique Lætitia,
I will not in this wilderness delay,
Where, without you, I am the one thing living,
Like some lone seaman left upon an island,
Who beats his head against an emptiness
And so goes mad.   Give me the knife!   I die.

> *(Stabs self and dies.   Chord.)*

PLUM. This is a most strange consequence and finish
Of one quite simple action——   Ho!   Without!

Enter WAITER.

Where are the officers of this Society?

WAITER. Sir, they are drinking.

PLUM.   Then disturb them not,
But with all speed call ministers and surgeons.
Reverently then these bodies disentangle,
And in two chambers decently dispose them,
Not in one vague and ill-considered heap,
As men store pheasants, cock and hen together,
But with due awe distinguishing the sexes.
And this poor body, which shall top the pile,
Cause in a cylinder to be cremated
Not far from Winchester, where I was born.
This is the end.   Go, fellow!   I have done.

WAITER. Sir, from my birth I was a nervous child,
This way and that swung weakly by suggestion,
And could not see my fellow-creatures weep
But I must echo them with noisy tears.
Speak of an earthquake, and I fly the house,
Hang o'er the bulwarks, I am sick myself.
And now, i' the presence of these diminished
   figures,
By their own act, I take it, brought to nought,
I feel the prickings of mortality.
Thoughts of destruction, fatal inclinations,
Throng in my arteries——

PLUM.   It is enough.
I see far off the goal to which you stumble.
Die and have done with it, for I am waiting.

                    (WAITER *knocks head thrice on
                         floor and dies.   Chord.*)

PLUM. Now do the morning and the evening meet

To kiss the midnight in the noon of death.

(Stabs self.   Music.)

Now is the circle of our questionings
Completed in an equilateral triangle,
Whereof like children in a labyrinth
At the perimeter we wander dumbly
Groping for truth, nor can one path discover
Which is not soon concluded in a point
That hath not magnitude, nor space, nor nothing,
But down the windy parallels of Time
Echoes again that interrogative
Which mocked our entrances. Now, Plum, go off !

(Stabs self.)

Now shall the night-hawk to the trees report,
" Plum is no more, poor Plum, that used to hang
High in the branches of authority,
Poor Plum is fallen from the bough unripened,
Shook off too soon by unkind circumstance."

(Stabs self.)

Now Popes and persons, majesties and powers,
Dominions, sunsets, Kings and macaroons,
Violets, marigolds, and moonlight falling
Like children's kisses on the mountain-top,

(Stabs self.)

Dukes, ferns, and shell-fish, and all gentle things
In the high argument of love suspended,
Firelight at evening and the dawn of day,
Red wings and walnuts, oak, mahogany,
Lancaster, York, great Salisbury, and Monmouth,
Hereford, Leicester, Northumberland, and Kent,
King's Cross, St. Pancras, Euston, Waterloo—
All noble-sounding and capacious words,

Come and be mourners at my funeral,
For I am in the vestibule of death,   (*Stabs self.*)

This is the gate and portal of my ending.
I think there doth not any word remain,
But silence and still quiet touch my lips
With the mute harmony of things unspoken.
I never was of that loud company
Which seek their harvest in a waste of words;
" Do " was my dictionary.   And my sword
Leaped from the sheath ere I could mention it.
                              (*Stabs self.*)

As you may see in some great orchestra,
A little lonely fellow at the end
Sits by the cymbals, and the instruments
Thunder around him their tempestuous din,
Flutes, horns, and oboes, harp, and clarinet,
And the wild fiddles like the forest swaying
On Swedish mountains when the storm is high.
But he, that could with one most royal clash

13

Startle the city, and make all that music
Like the small twittering of birds appear,
Sits with his brasses, but doth make no sound
Till the conductor shall command him so,
And leaves his cymbals and goes home at last,
Still with no sound, nor kindly thanks, nor notice,
For the conductor hath forgotten him—
So sit I here, and die without a word.

(Stabs self, and surveys scene.)

Well, this will puzzle them at Scotland Yard.

(Dies.   Chord.)

CURTAIN.

BALLADS FOR BROADBROWS

THE POODLE AND THE PUG

WHEN I was a High School noodle
  And life was rather smug,
My father kept a poodle,
  My mother kept a pug;
And every Sunday, after three,
This strange procession you might see,
My dear Papa, Mamma and me,
  The poodle and the pug.

The poodle I could never bear,
For he was naked here and there,
And, partly bare and partly hair,
  Was like a worn-out rug.
The pug, upon the other hand,
Was far too well upholstered, and
Somehow the pug I could not stand—
  I could not stand the pug.
Oh, dear, how I disliked those dogs!
The pug had features like a frog's,
And deep in the profoundest bogs
  Could I have put that pug.

For every Sunday, after three,
This strange procession you might see,
My dear Papa, Mamma and me,
    The poodle and the pug.

The poodle was alert and gay,
He liked to run in front and play
In quite a Continental way,
    Unlike the pompous pug ;
The pug was more the Saxon kind,
He plodded on a mile behind
And in his movements called to mind
    An alderman, or slug.
And that explains the life I led,
For it was I who, rather red,
Pursued the poodle, far ahead,
    Or waited for the pug.
And every Sunday, after three,
This strange procession you might see,
My dear Papa, Mamma and me,
    The poodle and the pug.

Those dogs have left their mark on me;
So many citizens I see
A sort of poodle seem to be,
    Or else a sort of pug.
At ballets of the Russian kind
Whole packs of poodles you will find,
With tufts of hair stuck here and there
    Which one would like to tug;
While as for pugs, if you reflect,
You know a dozen, I expect;
Well, Mrs. Bun at Number One
    Is definitely pug.
And you, when you go beddy-bye,
Look in your mirror, eye to eye,
And put the question, " Which am I—
    A poodle or a pug ?"

I cannot tell upon what grounds
I sing of these unpleasant hounds;
The Muse proceeds by leaps and bounds,
    One follows with a shrug.

But this is what occurs to me—
Degraded though the age may be,
At any rate we seldom see
   A poodle or a pug.
Our ways would make our fathers weep,
Our skirts too short, our drinks too deep;
But, dash it all, we do *not* keep
   A poodle or a pug!
And you, my child, will never be
Compelled on Sundays, after three,
To walk with your Mamma and me,
   A poodle and a pug.

OTHER PEOPLE'S BABIES

A Song of Kensington Gardens

Babies ? It's a gift, my dear; and I should say
  I know,
For I've been pushing prams about for forty years
  or so ;
Thirty-seven babies—or is it thirty-nine ?
No, I'm wrong ; it's thirty-six—but none of them
  was mine.
            Other people's babies—
                That's my life !
            Mother to dozens,
                And nobody's wife.
        But then it isn't everyone can say
        They used to bath the Honourable Hay,
    Lord James Montague, Sir Richard Twistle-Thynnes,
    Captain Cartlet and the Ramrod twins.
            Other people's babies,
                Other people's prams,
            Such little terrors,
                Such little lambs !
            Sixty-one today,
                And ought to be a granny ;
            Sixty-one today,
                And nothing but a Nanny !
                There, ducky, there,
                Did the lady stare ?
            Don't cry !   Oh, my !
                Other people's babies !

Everybody's told me, dear, since I was seventeen,
I ought to been a mother—what a mother I'd have
  been !
Mind you, minding babies isn't everybody's line,
But I wouldn't mind the minding, dear, if I was
  minding mine.

> *Other people's babies*
> *All my life—*
> *Three dozen mothers,*
> *And not one wife.*
> *Of course, it isn't everyone can say*
> *They used to bath the Honourable Hay,*
> *Lord Charles Cobley—had a present from the King—*
> *And now, they tell me, he's a Bright Young Thing.*
> *But forty years of bottles,*
> *Forty years of fits,*
> *Forty years of first teeth,*
> *And here I sits,*
> *Sixty-one today,*
> *Might have been a granny,*
> *Meant for a mother,*
> *And nothing but a Nanny !*
> *There, ducky, there,*
> *Howl if you dare*
> *Don't cry ! Oh, my !*
> *Other people's babies !*

Isn't he a pet, my dear—the spit of Lady Stoop ?
Looks a perfect picture, yes—I nursed him through
  the croup ;

But I shall get my notice just as soon as he can
  crawl—
It's a funny thing to think he won't remember me
  at all.

> *Other people's babies,*
> > *Nothing to show—*
> *Twelve months' trouble,*
> > *And out I go.*
> *Of course, it isn't everyone can say*
> *They used to bath the Honourable Hay,*
> *Lady Susan Sparrow, what was dropped in the pond,*
> *And now, Cook tells me, she's a well-known blonde.*
> > *But forty years of croup,*
> > > *Forty years of frights,*
> > *Long, long days, dear,*
> > > *And short, short nights—*
> > *Sixty-one today,*
> > > *And ought to be a granny.*
> > *Pensions for the widows, eh?*
> > > *But what about the Nanny?*
> > > *There, ducky, there,*
> > > *Nannies don't care!*
> > *Don't cry!   Oh, my!*
> > > *Other people's babies!*

NOCTURNE

This party is rather a bore;
I shall go to such parties no more.
    Will somebody kind
    My overcoat find
And quietly show me the door?

I'm weary of standing about,
Making silly remarks in a shout;
    The sandwiches taste
    Of photograph-paste,
And now the white wine has run out!
    I shall go to bed early tonight,
    I'm feeling a little bit done;
    But I like the young lady in white,
    And it's only a quarter to one.

Oh, why do we gather in herds,
Like a lot of excitable birds,
  And chatter and bawl
  About nothing at all
In wholly inaudible words?
There are seventy women and men
In this room, and it holds about ten.
  You heard what I said?
  I am going to bed,
And it's merely a question of " When ?"
 I shall go to bed early tonight,
  I'm feeling a little bit blue;
 But I like the young lady in white,
  And it's only a quarter to two.

There are too many people who write,
They're most of them present tonight;
  And how I abhor
  The musical bore
Who has collared the charmer in white!
And as for this girl with a mane,
She gives me a positive pain!
  She talks of James Joyce
  In a bronchial voice,
And I don't want to see her again.
 But I do like the lady in white,
  And I wish she was married to me.
 I shall go to bed early tonight—
  Oh, dear, it's a quarter to three!

There are too many people who paint;
It's becoming a chronic complaint;
  They're all of them here,
  They've finished the beer,
And I think I am going to faint.
But I've met the young lady in white;
Our talk was exciting but slight:
  " Good evening," she said,
  " I am going to bed;
So glad to have met you. Good-night!"
 Still, I've met the young lady in white,
  And I wish we had met a bit more.
 I shall go to bed early tonight—
  Oh, gosh! it's a quarter to four!

"REDUNDANT"

This old pub has got to go, they say,
     'Cos it's redundant.
Funny words they use for things today—
     What price "redundant"?
     Well, what I want to know,
     If a pub has got to go,
     There's no harm in saying so—
     But why "redundant"?

Redundant! Redundant! Well, what a silly word!
  " Superfluous," " A blot upon the scene,"
    " One too many"—see?
    It was all explained to me—
  But where's the harm in saying what you mean?
What's the use of all this education?
Heaven help the poor old British nation
    If the only word we know
    For a pub that's got to go
     Is redundant,
     Redundant,
Redundyundyundant!

But words like that is useful now and then—
     And so's redundant.
You couldn't have a better name for men—
     They're just redundant;
     Bill's acting very base,
     But you ought to see his face
     When I says with quiet grace,
     "'Ere, you're redundant."

Redundant! Redundant! Well, nothing calms him down
Like one of them big mouthfuls out of novels.

Tell him he's a brute
And he throws another boot,
But tell him he's redundant and he grovels.
There's something after all in education;
It helps you in an awkward situation.

If you can give a man the bird
With a perfect lady's word
    Like redundant,
    Redundant,
Redundyundyundyundyundant !

When you come to think the matter out,
    We're all redundant.
There's very few you couldn't do without—
    They're just " redundant";
    Well, look at Albert Fife,
    And look at Albert's wife!
    In fact, the whole of life
    'S a bit redundant.

Redundant !   Redundant !   Well, what a useful word !
    Seems to fit the neighbours like a glove,
      Likewise the little gent
      What comes about the rent,
    The Taxes and the Government and Love.
Life is one redundant complication
Asking for abrupt elimination.
      And what about your beer ?
      Get rid of it, my dear—
        It's redundant,
        Redundant,
    It's redundyundyundyundyundyundyundant !

THE VITAMINS

(A Scientific Song)

Vitamin " A "
Keeps the rickets away
And succours the meagre and nervy ;
" B "'s what you lack
If the stomach is slack,
And " C " is the foe of the scurvy ;
So when a man dines
Let him murmur these lines,
Or sure he will live to deplore it—
Just ask yourself " What
Disease have I got,
And which is the vitamin for it ?"

A doctor with a microscope
Was mixing mutton-fat and soap
When what was his surprise to see
A Thing invisible to me
(And I am quite prepared to bet
That no one else has seen it yet).
It showed upon its gentle face
Affection for the human race,
And it is very rare to find
An organism of this kind ;
So, with a microscopic grin,
He christened it a Vitamin.

There are three Vitamins, not four,
I have no doubt there will be more,*
But for the present you and me
Must do the best we can with three.
And Nelson, Raleigh, Drake, St. Paul,
Did fairly well with none at all.
These simple people never knew
The secrets shared by me and you;
No chemical analysis
Of this and that and that and this
Their hearty dinners did condemn—
They gobbled what was given them;
But this affects a man's inside,
And all these foolish fellows died.

But you and I, of sterner schools,
Must eat by scientific rules.
You may remember, as a kid,
A fuss about the Proteid,
And at (I think) a later stage
The Calories became the rage;
The Carbohydrates now and then
Have exercised the learned men,
And whether people took enough
Albuminous and starchy stuff;
For nothing, we may well conclude,
Is quite so dangerous as food—
In fact, before the doctors call
It's safest not to eat at all.

* Already (they tell me) this prophecy has been fulfilled.

It is my purpose here to state
That all these views are out of date,
And even surgeons now admit
The little Vitamin is It.
So do not plunge a hasty fork
Into the pickles or the pork,
But telephone to Harley Street,
" Is this a vital thing to eat ?"
Before you order what you want—
Tripe, caviare or crême de menthe—
Before you seize and swallow whole
Some luscious bird or fancy sole,
Send for the manager and hiss,
" Is there a Vitamin in this ?"

There are no Vitamins in lard,
From bacon they are wholly barred ;
In potted meat they are not seen,
Nor olive-oil nor margarine ;
In vain your families you cram
With coffee, cocoa, sugar, jam.
I very much regret to add
That tapioca's just as bad.
Nor do I know how we contrive
For years and years to keep alive
When most of what we eat and drink
Would be much better down the sink.

" A "

But courage !   In cod-liver oil
The healthy little creatures toil ;

And any backward child of mine
Who showed a softness in the spine
Should frequently be fed on that,
With good hard roes and bits of fat,

Fresh butter, cheese and yolk of egg,
Will fortify the infant leg,
For here again are found, they say,
Those vitamins we christen " A ";
In cabbage, too, and other greens,
And lettuces (but not in beans).

" B '

But better still for you and me,
Who are not children now, is " B ";
His duty, which he does not shirk,
Is just to make the stomach work.
If my supply of " B " is small
My liver does not act at all,
And things go on in my inside
Which never can be justified.

Those old philosophers and saints
Who had mysterious complaints
And perished on some lonely mount
In ways for which we can't account—
The explanation's clear to me,
They did not get enough of " B ".

Well, " B " occurs in nuts and peas,
In lentils, beans, and things like these,
In wholemeal rye and wholemeal wheat,
And bread which is not fit to eat,
In roes of fish and some dried fruits
And milk and yeast and uncooked roots;
And death, as far as I can see,
May be preferred to eating " B ".

" C "

But " C " is quite another thing,
Of " C " with frank delight I sing;
For " C " 's the pretty Vitamin
Who makes and mends that schoolgirl skin,
And stops it coming out in lots
Of horrid, horrid little spots.

" C " is the very best excuse
For drinking pints of orange-juice ;
For " C "'s sweet sake fine ladies feed
Upon the radish and the swede.

Tomatoes, salads, lemons, milk,
Keep noble skins as smooth as silk ;
The prettiest girl I ever saw
Ate cauliflower and rhubarb raw.
But best of all about him is
That " C " abounds in strawberries.

" D "

The doctors, I am glad to see,
Admit that there are none in tea ;
They worship, as I said before,
Three only ; but I know one more.

For I have found a Vitamin
In brandy, burgundy and gin;
And I salute with three times three
The little chap I know as " D."

Vitamin " A "
Keeps the rickets away
And succours the meagre and nervy;
" B " 's what you lack
If the tummy is slack,
And " C " is the foe of the scurvy:
And so when you dines
Remember these lines,
And, if you'll be guided by me, Sir,
It don't matter what
Disease you have got,
Just order a bottle of " D ", Sir.

" HUSH, MRS. HUNDRED, HUSH !"

Hush, Mrs. Hundred, hush—
   If that's all you've got to say !
A hundred centenarians
   In their gentle, courtly way
Have told us we're barbarians
   And rotten with decay.
We have no heart, she has no hair,
They powder their noses everywhere,
Their skirts are short, we cannot court.
   The younger generation
Have neither manners, pride nor grace,
There is no future for the race,
The modern girl is one long whirl,
   And Heaven help the nation.

Well, there she goes, my modern dear—
Is there no grace, old lady, here ?
So quick and neat, those feathered feet,
They walk the wind and not the street.
Old lady, did they walk so well
When you were young ? I cannot tell.
I know you could not show such legs—
Such twinkling, silken, silver legs—
That flash a challenge far away
(And mark you, Madam, in your day,
When Julia's legs might not be shown,
Her fortune was her face alone ;

But now the plainest Jane you know
May be a beauty down below):
   So hush, Mrs. Hundred, hush!
    Did you have legs as pretty?
  And if you did, and kept them hid,
    Why, Madam, what a pity!

    But look again!
    She is not plain.
"Ridiculous hat!" you said!
    Well, that may be,
    Still, one can see
The shape of that proud head.
The eyes, observe, are not cast down
As if she feared to face the town;
More human, Ma'am, and more divine,
Her honest eyes encounter mine,
Which, Madam, is what I prefer,
And if you don't, I think you err,
   So hush, Mrs. Hundred, hush!

    And then she's slim,
    So swift and slim,
  Electric wires in every limb!
And she can ride and she can swim,
And she can dance till the stars grow dim,
And, waking fresh as violets,
Play eighteen holes or seven sets,
    Or paint, or cook,
    Or write a book,
    Or fence, or vote,
    Or sail a boat,

Will run a mile or run a man
(And run the office if she can),
Defend a burglar, drive a 'plane,
And in the evening dance again;
    So hush, Mrs. Hundred, hush!
    Control yourself and ponder:
Should you have thrown that spiteful stone
    At my young lady yonder?

You did not show your ankles, no,
    And maybe that was wise,
For sitting about had puffed them out
    To such an awkward size.
You could not ride, you could not swim,
You could not dance till the stars grew dim,
And, waking fresh as violets,
Play eighteen holes or seven sets,
You could not run, you could not row,
You could do nothing much but sew,
You'd scarcely crawl across the hall
    Unless you were supported,
You fled the house at the sight of a mouse
    And swooned when you were courted.
And, Madam, have you always been
    So rare a judge of clothing?
Have you forgot the painful scene
When you put on your crinoline,
Your fashionable crinoline?
Like some balloon of bombazine
You floated round the croquet-ground,
    While Granny watched with loathing.

" Ridiculous dress!" I think she cried,
" Far, far too long and much too wide!
When I was that young woman's age
We wore a frock and not a cage,
  The girl's a perfect *sight*!
That crazy skirt collects the dirt!"
  And, Madam, she was right.

You don't know what we're coming to—
    No more did she.
There are not many, Ma'am, who do,
    But, as you see,
At present we're an inch or two
    Below the knee;
And I confess I like it so—
Look, Ma'am, again.   And then, you know,
  Skirts always will be wrong,
  Too short or else too long;
  Yet England's going strong,
    Take it from me.

  Hush, Mrs. Hundred, hush!
    You are a dear,
  But hush, Mrs. Hundred, hush!
    I will not hear.
  Hush, Mrs. Hundred, hush!
    Your song is sung;
  But not so long ago
    You were the Modern Young.

FOUR NEGRO COMMERCIALS

1. DERE AIN'T NO WIMMIN . . .

DERE ain't no wimmin in Hebb'n,
Dere ain't no wimmin in Hebb'n,
An' dis nigger ain't a-goin' to Hebb'n,
  'Cos I'm fixed on meetin' my Mammy.

Yo' Mammy nussed you from a little child,
              Jem Johnson,
An' you saw Hebb'n when yo' Mammy smiled,
              Jem Johnson,

  But dere ain't no wimmin in Hebb'n.
  No, dere ain't no wimmin in Hebb'n, etc.

I hear de good ole preacher say,
              Jem Johnson,
You buy no mo' shoes for Martha Gray,
              Jem Johnson,
  'Cos dere ain't no wimmin in Hebb'n.
  Oh, dere ain't no wimmin in Hebb'n,
  An' dis nigger ain't a-goin' to Hebb'n,
  'Cos I'm fixed on meetin' my Mammy.

2. PLAY ON YO' HARP

It's no use niggers t'inkin' dey's white—
      Play on yo' harp, Ole Nigger !
It's no use takin' dem powders at night—
      Play on yo' harp, Ole Nigger.

Put dem fancy petticoats down,
You got a harp an' I got a crown,
An', Lord, who'll care if youse black or brown,
    Playin' on yo' harp, Ole Nigger?

You'll never be President of de United States—
    Play on yo' harp, Ole Nigger!
But you'll come first at de Golden Gates—
    Play on yo' harp, Ole Nigger!
Hey, gal, don't you powder yo' face!
What d'you want wid ribbons and lace?
You'll look fine in de angels' place
    Playin' on yo' harp, Ole Nigger!

3. DAT BUTTERFLY

Don't strike dat butterfly, Nigger,
    He's got wings, like you.
      Dat butterfly
      Am goin' to die,
    Same as you an' same as I ;
      But you and I
      Am goin' to fly
    Same as dat dam butterfly ;
So don't strike dat butterfly, Nigger,
    He's got wings, like you.

All togeder in de upper air,
You an' me an' de Great Black Bear,
All good chillun will be flyin' up dere—
    Don't strike dat butterfly, Nigger,
      He's got wings, like you, etc.

An' it don't matter how you try,
Hidin' in de corners all around de sky,
You'm sure to meet dat butterfly.
Don't strike dat butterfly, Nigger,
He's got wings like you, etc.

Dat butterfly den he up and say,
" Hey, you done strike me, one fine day!"
An' Peter, he take yo' harp away.
So don't strike dat butterfly, Nigger,
He's got wings like you-oo, etc.

4. STOWAWAY

Stowaway ! Stowaway !
I see you hidin';
Stowaway ! Stowaway !
Come out of yo' corner.
Stowaway ! Stowaway !
I'se rowin' dis boat,
I'se rowin' dis boat,
I'se rowin' dis boat,
An' you can't go over Jordan,
You can't cross over Jordan today,
Stowaway !

THE POWDER MONKEYS

Whenever we can
  We powder the nose;
What worries a man
  Like a luminous nose?
In sickness or health,
In woe or in wealth,
But never by stealth,
  We powder the nose.

The brush and the comb,
  The care of the nose,
Were kept for the home,
  We used to suppose;
But now there's no place
Where it's a disgrace
To attend to the face
  As soon as it glows.

397   14

He loses control,
  We powder the nose;
He pours out his soul,
  We powder the nose;
To boredom or bliss
Our answer is this;
A curse—or a kiss?—
  We powder the nose.

Our lovers depart,
  We powder the nose;
They shatter the heart,
  We powder the nose;
The enemy's nigh,
We melt and we cry,
But our powder is dry
  And we see to the nose.

What use is the dress,
  The hat or the hose,
If there's an excess
  Of shine on the nose?

Godiva could dare
To go about bare;
The girl didn't *care*—
   She'd powdered the nose.

We'll stand in the dock
   And powder the nose,
And if to the block
   We finally goes
The procession will lag
While we open the bag,
Extract the last fag,
   And powder the nose.

A SONG OF THE NORTH

THEY'VE stopped the band from playing in the Park
On a Sunday;
They close the Public Gardens after dark
On a Sunday;
This town's a tomb and no mistake;
The Borough Council wins the cake;
It seems a sin to be awake
On a Sunday.

Nowhere to go,
Nowt to be done,
Mustn't hear music,
Mustn't have fun;
The pictures are shut and we haven't no club,
The only thing open this evening's the pub.
And, oh, my! we're ready to cry
As we walk up and down
This nice pious town,
On a dreary, drizzly,
Granny's own grisly,
Muddy, municipal Sunday.

It's difficult to court a girl, you see,
On a Sunday,
If her dear mother hides the parlour-key
On a Sunday.

Well, it's not easy to be sweet
When a couple's only chance to meet
Is in a shower, in the street,
   On a Sunday.

 Nowhere to go,
  Nowhere to kiss,
   Mustn't do that,
    And mustn't do this.
But there's the Museum, and there without fail
We hug in a corner behind a stuffed whale ;
 But, oh, my ! the keepers do pry,
  And often I wish
  There was some bigger fish
  On a dreary, drizzly,
  Granny's own grisly,
Mouldy, municipal Sunday.

They've stopped the band from playing in the Park
   On a Sunday,
For Mendelssohn seemed too much like a lark
   On a Sunday ;
 They've stopped the music in the Park,
 They chase the couples after dark,
 But dogs is still allowed to bark
   On a Sunday.

  Nowhere to sit,
   Walk up and down,
   Mustn't hear music
    In this pious town.

The Mayor thinks *Handel* is bad for my soul,
But he's playing golf—at the nineteenth hole;
And, oh, my! I'm ready to cry:
  I've blistered my feet
  Walking the street
    On a dreary, drizzly,
    Granny's own grisly,
Moral, municipal Sunday.

SONG FOR THE PARENTS OF YOUNG THINGS INTENT ON MARRYING THE WRONG PEOPLE

You young things who hurry to wed are a worry,
   You make me exceedingly wild;
We all want our ration of flowery passion,
   But that isn't marriage, my child.
I don't want to hear about Eros's dart;
You're not in a grand operatical part;
And when you refer to the gentleman's heart,
   I ask myself, " What are his hobbies ?"
       " What's his hobby, dear ?"
        My father used to say.
      Is it bigamy or beer ?
        Could you stand him all the day ?
      Kisses, I allow,
      Are the main thing now,
  But marriage isn't one protracted Maytime.
      Love's all right
      By artificial light,
  But none of you seem to think about the daytime.

It isn't enough to be rather hot stuff
   By the light of the silvery moon;
Any fool can excite on a Saturday night,
   But what about Monday at noon?

With lip close to lip any girl can impress,
But to see eye to eye is the test of success
When she wants to Charleston and you to play
  Chess,
  Just ask yourself, "What are her hobbies?"

"What's her hobby, please?"
  My father used to say.
Is her bonnet full of bees?
  Could you stand her all the day?
How will you feel
At the morning meal?

Marriage isn't one protracted Maytime.
  Love's all right
  By artificial light,
But none of you seem to think about the daytime.

It's not the remark which is made in the dark,
  But the things which are hissed at the table.
Well, what has been said about reading in bed?
  And do you suppose you'll be able?
Her eyes may be angel's—but what of her skull?
He may be a devil—but will he be *dull*?
Well, how would you stand a wet Sunday at Hull?
  I want to know, "What are his hobbies?"
    "*What's his hobby, dear?*"
      My father used to say.
    Is it bigamy or beer?
      Could you stand him all the day?
    Kisses, I allow,
    Are the main thing now,
But marriage isn't one protracted Maytime.
  Love's all right
  By artificial light,
But none of you seem to think about the daytime.

FOREIGN POLICY; OR, THE UNIVERSAL AUNT

I'm tired of Lithuania,
    I weary of the Lett,
I never had no mania
    For Pole or Prussian yet;
Old England is an island,
    And this is my complaint,
Why does Old England mess about
    With continents which ain't?

Poor old Britannier, the Universal Aunt!
Think that you can mother everybody? Well, you can't.
What d'you want with Europe? Why d'you wish to
    roam?
Ain't you got enough misfortunes in the home?

The foreigner's an alien,
    He does not rule the waves;
Give me the good Australian
    Who cleans his teeth and shaves.
Oh, let the hairy Magyar
    Stew in his horrid juice,
And scrap the Foreign Office,
    For it ain't no kind of use!

Poor old Britannier! Talk about disarm?
It's these here diplomatists that do the greatest harm.
Scrap the Foreign Office! Why d'you want to roam?
Ain't you got enough misfortunes in the home?

The paper's all Croatians
  And Jugo-Slavs and Czechs,
In all these bearded nations
  We're buried to the necks;
But it takes a flood or earthquake
  Or other nasty mess
To get the British Empire
  Into the British Press!

Poor old Britannier!   Excuse a little sob;
Ain't your far-flung Empire a whole-time job?
Less of this Locarny-blarney!   Why d'you want to
  roam?
Ain't you got enough misfortunes in the home?

THE DREADFUL BALLAD OF A TALKIE-RUINED HOME

A MOTHER stood in tears amid the ruins of her home
Beseeching of her menfolk dear that evening not to roam;
Her first-born rose and struck her, but as he reached the door
The woman on her bended knees her husband did implore—

> *" Don't take my boy to the Talkies!*
> *It's puttin' ideas in 'is 'ead,*
> *'E makes the most 'orrible faces,*
> *And sleeps with a gun in 'is bed.*
> *'E uses outlandish American words,*
> *It's nothin' but " bootleggers," " babies," and " birds,"*
> *'E says I've an English accent*
> *An' it's not that I mind the snub,*
> *But I want my boy to be British,*
> *So take 'im with you to the pub!"*

Out passed the men together to the gilded pleasure-hall
To feast their eyes on " Passion Buds "—or " Love Excuses All."
And crooks and crimes and cabarets, and girls in dishabille,
While on the lonely kitchen-floor the mother murmured still—

" Don't take my boy to the Talkies!
It's them that has poisoned the lad.
Don't let 'im talk through 'is nose, dear,
I'd sooner 'e went to the bad.
Don't let 'im talk like the Talkies, you see,
Why can't 'e speak the King's English, like me?
'E tells me I ain't got no sex-urge,
And it's not that I mind the snub,
But I want my boy to be pu-ure,
So take 'im with you to the pub!"

The show was done, the boy said " Dad, I gotter kill
   ternight!
I feel the blood-lust in my bones."   His father said
   " That's right."
They robbed a passing postman then, and, home
   again once more,
They murdered that poor woman, but she whispered
   through her gore—

" Don't take my boy to the Talkies !
I told you it done 'im no good.
Now we'll be all in the papers,
And all through that there 'Ollywood.
Tell the kind judge that the boy ain't to blame,
Ever since " Broadway " 'e's not been the same.
'E told me I'm Nobody's Baby,
And it's not that I mind the snub,
But I want my boy to be British,
So take 'im with you to the pub !"

NEWS: A BALLAD FOR BREAKFAST-TIME

THERE'S not very much in the paper,
  But what's in the paper is bad,
A peeress has married a draper,
  An aeroplane's crashed at Bagdad.
A girl has been cruelly battered,
  She was battered to death with a bat,
The authorities say that it points to foul play,
  And what do you think of that?

> *News! News! It gives you the blues,*
> *Slaughters of daughters and all the clues!*
> *Why do we peruse the discouraging news*
> *On a mouldy Monday morning?*

There's been a big fire in Australia,
  And a small revolution in Spain;
They're growing a new kind of dahlia;
  The Government's blundered again.
A woman has flown the Atlantic
  And explained to the Press in a chat
That she'd not the remotest idea she'd be noticed—
  And what do you think of that?

> *News! News! Neurotical news!*
> *Publicity Cissy she gives me the blues;*
> *But I can't refuse a nice bit of news*
> *On a mouldy Monday morning.*

411

Our trade is deplorably groggy,
   A bad epidemic is near,
The forecast is " Freezing and Foggy,"
   They think you get cancer from beer.
A lady who's nearly a hundred
   Sees ladies she's horrified at,
And she wouldn't wonder if England went under—
   And that, says the lady, is that.

> *News ! News ! Nonsensical news !*
> *Fashions and passions you can't excuse,*
> *But I wouldn't lose my bit of bad news*
> *On a mouldy Monday morning.*

Unless I am greatly mistaken
   We've all of us plenty to do ;
Why must we absorb with our bacon
   The woes of the Universe too ?
For breakfast the crisis at Koosh-Koosh,
   For lunch the disaster at Kat,
Some other man's winner at tea, and at dinner
   A murder or two. And that's that.

> *News ! News ! It gives you the blues,*
> *Sinners and winners and why they lose ;*
> *But everyone chews his bit of bad news*
> *On a mouldy Monday morning.*

And often I think of transferring
   To some less excitable zone
Where not very much is occurring,
   And that is not publicly known ;

Where flights are conducted in secret,
    And people would not care a drat
If a typist went frantic and *swam* the Atlantic—
    And that, since you ask me, is that.

> *News! News! Oh for a snooze!*
> *Slaughters of daughters and all the clues,*
> *Dramas, pyjamas and drugs and booze,*
> *Arsons and parsons and all their views,*
> *Smashes and crashes that don't amuse!*
> *News! News! I'd like to vamoose*
> *Anywhere, anywhere out of the news,*
> *But meanwhile I glues my nose to the news*
>   *Every mouldy morning.*

MR. BAEDEKER: OR, BRITONS ABROAD

In duty bound
We've tottered round
From gallery to gallery;
And seeing sights
We think by rights
Deserves a handsome salary.

Our necks are stiff from staring up at ornamental
roofs,

We've masterpieces on the brain and blisters on the
hoofs,

We've peered at bits of tapestry and pottery and
wood,

And looked them up in catalogues to see if they
were good;

For Kings and Governments may err,
But never Mr. Baedeker.
And by degrees we mean to look
At everything that's in his book;
What he admired
We mean to see,
But we're very, very tired,
And we want a cup of tea.

Oh, Mr. Baedeker! We've reached page four,
And Oh, Mr. Baedeker, we can't do any more.
Say what you will, Sir, the finest sight
Is our rock-garden on a moonlit night.

It's hard to say
Why in this way
We occupy our little ease ;
We don't much care
For porcelain ware
Or sculpture by Praxiteles :
But we are not here for pleasure, and a man must
keep in touch
With works of art by foreigners which bore him
very much,

With ivories and vases and Napoleonic beds,
With heads which have no bodies and with busts
which haven't heads ;
We've conscientiously tabooed
All statuary in the nude,
But shown a proper interest
In figures adequately dressed :

What he admired
　　We mean to see,
But we're very, very tired,
　　And we want a cup of tea.
Oh, Mr. Baedeker!　We've done this town,
And Oh, Mr. Baedeker, we must sit down.
Say what you will, Sir, the finest sight
Is our rock-garden on a moonlit night.

PHILOSOPHY

How are you, Milly ?   As for me,
  Oh, well, we mustn't grumble ;
Things isn't what they used to be,
  But there, we mustn't grumble ;
Poor Albert's out of work again,
My Lizzie's got her favourite pain,
And don't it make you sick, this rain ?
  But there, we mustn't grumble.

It's no use hollering until you're burning,
  It's an ill wind that don't blow no one good,
It's a long lane that hasn't any turning ;
  I've got my health and spirits—touching wood.
We oughter won a thousand pounds from that there
  Guessing Game,
I guessed the horses right enough and Albert sent the claim,
And now it seems he's been and gone and never signed
  his name !
  But there, we mustn't grumble,

The landlord's playing up a treat,
  But there, we mustn't grumble.
Well, says he'll turn us on the street ;
  But there, we mustn't grumble ;
Of course, what I'd put by is spent,
And all I've got to pay the rent
Is twopence—one of which is bent,
  But there, we mustn't grumble.

417

I never hold with worrying and whining,
  Well, what I say is what must be must be,
And every cloud has got a silver lining,
  Though now and then it's very hard to see.
These little things are only sent to try us, don't they say ?
Poor Albert's been to Epsom backing winners all the day,
And every time his horse came in, his bookie went away—
  But there, we mustn't grumble.

So Maud's expecting ?   Is that so ?
  Oh, well, we mustn't grumble.
Six is a lot—I ought to know—
  But there, we mustn't grumble.
There's one or two with eight or nine,
There's some as sits and sips their wine
And wish they'd had a few of mine—
  So there, we mustn't grumble.

It might be snowing if it wasn't raining ;
  We've plenty to be thankful for, I mean.
When Albert starts his cursing and complaining
  I always say " Well, look what might have been !"
They're taking all my teeth out, but the dentist's very kind,
Well, what I say, we might have all been deaf and dumb and blind,
And we've never had the house on fire, that I can call to mind,
  So there, we mustn't grumble.

MUMPS

(A Merry Christmas Song)

My wife, poor thing, has got the mumps,
Her neck is just a lot of lumps.
Her Christmas she will spend in bed,
Consuming gruel, milk and bread;
      And it is cruel
      To play with gruel
When turkeys are the trumps;
      I say it's crule
      To spend one's Yule
In quarantine for Mumps.

My wife has gone and got the mumps,
The family is in the dumps;
It would enrage a plaster saint
To get this infantile complaint
      At Christmas-time
      When birds are prime
And off go all our humps;
      I say it's hard
      To be debarred
From merriment by mumps.

What is the use of doctors who
Know all the things that doctors do,
Can draw a complicated plan
Of what goes on inside a man

And tell what's best
For someone's chest
With three well-chosen thumps,
But in a case
Of swollen face
Can only say " It's mumps "?

Has Science with impartial pride
Mapped out the stars and my inside,
Yet cannot obviate or check
A silly swelling in the neck?
Why such conceit
In Harley Street?
What are their stomach-pumps,
Their diets, dopes
And stethoscopes?
They cannot stop the mumps!

But we will garlands to her bring,
Hang holly round the bed and sing
" Oh, may the man who gave her mumps
Be wed to five successive frumps!
Oh, may his stocks
Take nasty knocks
In all the Wall Street slumps!"
For it is crule
To spend one's Yule
In quarantine for mumps.

LET'S STOP SOMEBODY FROM DOING SOMETHING!

Councillor Busy and Mr. Nose, the Member for
    Misery Wood,
And the Secretaree for the Societee for Making the
    Public Good,
Were walking up and down the town with a frown,
    for everywhere they saw
The bold, bad Britisher doing things which weren't
    against the law;
    And "This won't do!" said Councillor Busy;
    "This won't do!" said the Honourable Nose;
    "It certainly won't!" said the Secretaree of the
    S.M.B.P.G.

" Let's stop somebody from doing something !
        Everybody does too much.
  People seem to think they've a right to eat and drink,
  Talk and walk and respirate and rink,
        Bicycle and bathe and such.
    So let's have lots of little regulations,
    Let's make laws and jobs for our relations,
    There's too much kissing at the railway stations—
  Let's find out what everyone is doing,
        And then stop everyone from doing it."

Councillor Busy and Mr. Nose walked on through
    the summer night,
And a young man looked at his lady friend and
    suddenly smiled outright;

And he hadn't applied for a licence, or been to the
   County Hall,
Or made a report at the magistrate's court, or filled
   up a form at all;
   And " Did you see that ?" said Councillor Busy ;
   " Did you see *that* ?" said the Honourable Nose ;
   " I *did* see that," said the Secretaree of the
   S.M.B.P.G.

" Let's stop somebody from doing something !
            There's too much smiling in the city.
   You don't see me in conversation with a she ;
   We don't osculate, and why should he ?
            Send for the Watch Committee !
      Let's make the girls wear high-necked blouses,
      Let's put microphones in people's houses,
      Let's imprison gentlemen who hug their spouses ;
   Let's find out what everyone is doing,
            And then stop everyone from doing it."

Councillor Busy went up to Heaven (from eating too
   much fruit),
And the Secretaree took an overdose of tea, and
   Nose soon followed suit ;
But they didn't much like the tone of Heaven, for
   the tone was far too gay.
The angels seemed to enjoy themselves, and the
   young folk laughed all day.
   And " This won't do," said Councillor Busy ;
   " Did you see *that* ?" said the Honourable Nose ;
   " No self-control !" said the Secretaree of the
   S.M.B.P.G.

" *Let's stop somebody from doing something !*
  There's too much liberty here,
  Constant song is obviously wrong,
  Let's get a plainclothes constable along—
            Somebody should interfere.
    Let's stop love and lollipops and smoking,
    Let's stamp out unregulated joking,
    We've got noses and they're made for poking,
  Let's find out what everyone is doing,
          And then stop everyone from doing it."

VERSES FOR EVERY DAY

BREAKFAST

GIVE me a little ham and egg
And let me be alone, I beg.
Give me my tea, hot, sweet and weak;
Bring me *The Times* and do not speak.
Let it at once be understood
My night was very far from good;
I say, I did not sleep a wink
Till half-past five or six, I think,
And then, of course—another cup?—
The birds began and woke me up;
At any rate, till after ten
I shall not love my fellow-men.
Till then it will be much the best
If no one here attempts to jest;
And do not let my lusty young
In my vicinity give tongue.
If Baby has to throw his ball,
Then let him throw it in the hall.
Let none with hearty tones enthuse,
But let me wallow in the news—
Distress, divorces, fire and flood,
Foul murder, bigamy and blood—
Such grim events befit the meal,
For that's exactly how I feel.
Address me softly after ten,
I shall be conscious, dear, by then;

But now my tea, hot, sweet and weak—
Give me *The Times* and do not speak.

To a Wrong Number

No, Sir, I am not Mr. Dark,
Nor am I Kensington, but Park:
My number, too, is quite unique,
And most unlike the one you seek.
Yes, yes, it hurts you, I can see,
And frankly, it's a blow to me;
For I was shaving when you rang,
And down three flights of stairs I sprang.
(You will not take offence, I hope,
If what I say is largely soap?
I'm out of breath, and I must own
There's soap upon the telephone.)
Where was I?   Well, the saddest thing—
I was expecting Jean to ring,
And when I heard the thrilling bell
I cut myself—I flew—I fell.
I take it you did not rejoice
To hear my cultivated voice;
Imagine, then, how one deplores
In such a case the sound of yours.
But there it is, and here we are,
So near, old fellow, yet so far.
Fate, that incorrigible wag,
Has dipped her fingers in the bag,
And, careless what the end may be—
Hullo?—connected you and me,
Two voices crying in the night,
Two dogs that bark but cannot bite.

Hullo?   But must this be the end?
Tell me about yourself, my friend.
Who are you?   How—and what—d'you do?
And are you Kensington or Kew?
Did you, as I did, hope to hear
The melting tones of someone dear?
What is her name?   And are you there?
And is she kind as she is fair?
Did she accept you or refuse?
Is she your lovely wife—or whose?
Or was it not a girl at all,
But some degrading business-call?
Your voice is hot with high affairs—
Don't tell me you are selling shares.
Ah, Sir, give up the chase for gold;
It's disappointing, so I'm told;
However spacious the amounts,
Love is the only thing that counts.
Ring off?   Ring *off*?   I can't think why.
However, if you must—Goodbye.
A pity.   But I shan't complain;
They're sure to put you through again.

COURTEOUS REPLY TO A MONEYLENDER'S CIRCULAR

LARGE-HEARTED Sir, I will allow
I *am* in need of money now;
But how have you the face to quote
The paltry figures in your note?
You do not seem to be aware
You have addressed a millionaire.

What is this talk of fifties, fool?
I think in thousands as a rule:
The present business I am at
Involves a larger sum than that.
You ask for no (I understand)
Security but note-of-hand,
While there should be, from what you say,
Almost no interest to pay:
And, if I read your offer right,
I'd like a million by tonight.

To the Head-Waiter at the ——

I LIKE the bow with which you wish
For my approval of the fish,
The lovely bird, so richly browned,
Which little sausages surround,
And dainty curls of bacon quite
Enough to make an appetite.
I love the proud but anxious smirk
That seems to say " An artist's work ";
I love to note your lighter mood
When I consent to eat the food;
But I have often wondered what
Would happen, friend, if I did not.
Let us experiment today—
Pray take the nasty bird away!
I never met such dreadful meat—
My hat, it is not fit to eat!

15

To a Junior Waiter

I KNOW I look the kind of dolt
Who never would or could revolt,
A martyr who prefers to wait
For food to blossom on his plate.
It's true I hate to make a scene,
Especially in front of Jean;
But, waiter, when I am upset
I am the fiercest fellow yet;
Quite suddenly I tear my hair
And leave the building then and there,
Employing rude expressions such
As would enrage you very much;
And from that moment I go on
And on about the Restaurant.
It's true I hate to make a scene,
Especially in front of Jean,
But there'll be one this afternoon,
If something doesn't happen soon.

At the Theatre

To the Lady Behind Me

DEAR Madam, you have seen this play;
I never saw it till today.
You know the details of the plot,
But, let me tell you, I do not.
The author seeks to keep from me
The murderer's identity,
And you are not a friend of his
If you keep shouting who it is.

The actors in their funny way
Have several funny things to say,
But they do not amuse me more
If you have said them just before;
The merit of the drama lies,
I understand, in some surprise;
But the surprise must now be small
Since you have just foretold it all.
The lady you have brought with you
Is, I infer, a half-wit too,
But I can understand the piece
Without assistance from your niece.
In short, foul woman, it would suit
Me just as well if you were mute;
In fact, to make my meaning plain,
I trust you will not speak again.
And—may I add one human touch?—
Don't breathe upon my neck so much.

To a Late-comer

I KNOW—I know how penitent you are;
You have had trouble with your awful car.
No fault of yours, but Circumstance and Fate,
Malign conspirators, have made you late.
You went and dressed in ample time, I know;
Your wife, of course, your watch as well, was slow;
You left the tickets on the mantel-shelf,
And the self-starter could not start itself;
As for the traffic, this was hard to beat,
You took an hour from Sloane to Regent Street.
Your dinner seemed a simple one, but still
It took an age—they would not bring the bill;

And then the women vanished, I suppose,
And spent ten minutes powdering the nose.
Then round Soho you drove, round Leicester Square
Policemen yelling " You must not park there !"
Anchored at last at Kew or Chorley Wood
And trotted here as quickly as you could.
And now, poor chap, you crawl from knee to knee ;
It hurts you just as much as it hurts me,
I know—I know—I know—I *know*—I KNOW!
But would you much mind getting off my toe?

THE ORIGIN OF SPECIES

I DO not lie awake till morn,
    As these professors do,
And wonder whether Man was born
    At Eden or the Zoo.
Did Man begin like you and me
Or climbing round the family tree,
A Gugnunc or a Chimpanzee?
    Well, I confess I'm neutral.

    I don't seem to care
    What my ancestors were—
It don't seem to matter to me.
    Perhaps they had tails,
    And perhaps they were snails,
Or something washed up by the sea;

Perhaps the professors are right when they claim
That Man is a monkey grown more or less tame,
But whatever they settle my rent is the same,
  So it don't seem to matter to me.

The learned men grow more and more
  Excitable and wan,
Enquiring what the world is for,
  And how it all goes on.
Is Life a little or a lot ?
Is Space a substance or a spot ?
Am I an accident, or what ?
    Well, I confess I'm neutral.

  I don't seem to care
  What my origins were—
Well, it don't seem to matter to me.
  The reason we're here
  Isn't perfectly clear,
But we're here for some time, I can see.
And Science in many things may be behind—
The improvement of beer is the one in my mind ;
But did the poor monkey descend from Mankind ?
  Well, it don't seem to matter to me.

I get no kick, I know not why,
  When men explain to me
There may be worlds beyond the sky
  Which I shall never see.
Six hundred million miles away
There may be life, or not, they say ;
It may be gravel soil, or clay ;
    And I confess I'm neutral.

Are there people in Mars?
Have they oysters and bars?
Well, it don't seem to matter to me.
For better, for worse,
I've took this Universe,
And the others can frizzle, for me.
I eat a good dinner, I earn a good pay,
I've a bob on a greyhound, I've chickens that lay,
And I'm taking my Jane to the pictures today,
So it don't seem to matter to me.

WHAT IS LOVE?

"WHAT is Love?" the poets question,
  And their answers don't impress;
But if they have no suggestion
  You and I can give a guess.
What is Love, that makes us gay
In this idiotic way?
Well, I'll whisper if I may—
    What is Love?
      A perfect nuisance.

What is Love?   It's Nature's blunder.
  What is Love?   A waste of time.
What is Love?   A nine days' wonder.
  What is Love?   The cause of crime.
   What is Lo-o-o-o-ove?
   What is Lo-o-o-o-ove?
What is Love?   A perfect nuisance—
   But I love you.

What is Love, that, swift or slowly,
  Brings all mortals to their knees?
Is it horrid?   Is it holy?
  Is it some obscure disease?
What is Love, that, Jew or Turk,
Lord or lackey, makes us shirk
Duty, Family and Work?
    What is Love?
      A public nuisance.

What is Love ?   A kind of measles.
What is Love ?   The end of sense.
What is Love ?   The cause of weasels.
What is Love ?   A great expense.
What is Lo-o-o-o-ove ?
What is Lo-o-o-o-ove ?
What is Love ?   A certain loser—
But I love you.

What is Love, that, with no warning,
Makes a fairy of a fright,
Takes a man that's sane this morning
And he's mad tomorrow night ?
What is Love, that saps our forces,
Makes us drink and bet on horses,
Ends in murders, debts, divorces ?
What is Love ?
A general nuisance.

What is Love ?   Creation's error.
What is Love ?   A source of crime.
What is Love ?   The sailor's terror.
What is Love ?   A waste of time.
What is Lo-o-o-o-ove ?
What is Lo-o-o-o-ove ?
What is Love ?   Well, that's what Love is—
But I love you.

I'VE GOT THE GIGGLES TODAY

A NICE young man about the town
Was long in love with Mary Brown,
And one fine day proposed to crown
    His lengthy adoration ;
But as he fell upon his knee
Exceedingly surprised was he
To hear her shout with girlish glee
    This chilling observation—

" I've got the giggles today !
    Everything's making me laugh ;
Once in a while I like a good smile—
    Today I'm too tickled by half.
Don't think it's anything personal, please,
But really you do look a fool on your knees !
    I see it was rude of me now,
    But I suddenly thought of a cow,
    Well, a rather nice calf—
    Oh, don't make me laugh,
For I've got the giggles today !"

Sweet Mary took her favourite car
And drove it very fast and far ;
Wherever dangerous corners are
    The little monster snorted ;
A constable his hand inclined,
But Mary bumped him from behind,
And when he mildly spoke his mind
    She laughingly retorted—

"*I've got the giggles today!*
Surely you understand that?
Doesn't life seem to be rather a scream?
How can you stand there in that hat?
I noticed your signal and thought I should burst—
You were just like the statue of Edward the First!
You can't think how funny you look!
The moment I saw you I shook.
Don't be a Dean,
You know what I mean—
I have got the giggles today!"

Poor Mary! As the years flew past
Her mirth grew more ill-timed and vast,
But Albert stuck it, and at last
He led her to the altar:
And when the parson murmured low
The words which all young women know
She quivered like a jelly-o
And smilingly did falter—

"*I've got the giggles today!*
It's really too funny to miss
Mother in tears! And how many years
Has Mother been living for this?
I've only just noticed that Albert is fat,
And why do the clergy wear collars like that?
Oh, hold me or else I shall fall—
I'll never be married at all!
'Obey,' did you say?
Please take me away
For I've got the giggles today!"

Poor Mary's married life was short,
A rumpus of a painful sort,
And then they questioned in the Court
    Her matrimonial fitness ;
But when the lawyer sought to pry
Exactly what she'd done and why
This most unsuitable reply
    Was uttered by the witness—

" *I've got the giggles today !*
    And you're such a master of chaff ;
I cannot recall what happened at all
    Because you keep making me laugh.
Well, why do you wear those ridiculous bibs ?
I'm going home now, for it's hurting my ribs.
    Of course, you were born at the Bar,
    You don't know how funny you are !
        Some other time
        We'll chat about crime,
    But I've got the giggles today !"

IS THAT CHAMPAGNE?

Is that champagne?
Then put it down the drain!
It's a taste that I'm unable to explain.
It picks you up, I know, but then it knocks you down
again;
I'd rather have some arrowroot, I'd rather have some rain;
Pour me out a crême de menthe, or something from
the main.
Is that champagne?
Then you can put it down the drain.

Unnatural compound, which, like some morass,
All day expels carbonic acid gas,
Fit but for weddings (and disgusting then)—
Take it away! This is no drink for men.

Is that champagne?
Then put it down the drain!
I never want to touch the stuff again.

442

Load me up with liquids of almost any sort—
Lemonade or liquorice or peppermint or port,
A nice light lager or a sherry if you're short,
         But, if that's champagne,
           Better put it down the drain.

Vile effervescence, bubbly though you be,
Mere aëration has no charms for me.
Still wines run deep ; give me a vintage red,
Which to the soul proceeds and not the head.

         Is that champagne ?
           Then put it down the drain !
         It's bogus and it's bilious, it's a bane.
Forty bob a bottle !   Well, it may amuse a peer ;
Some would take to water if the price of it was dear,
But who'd buy bubbly if it cost the same as beer ?
         Still, if that's champagne
           You can fill my glass again.

THE MOSCOW MANNER

In olden days, when someone wanted something of
  another,
He spoke him fair and friendly as a Briton and a
  brother;
And persons who desired their troops to hurry to the
  fray
Were careful to suggest it in a complimentary way,
Singing—

> Yeomen! True men! Sons of the free!
> Heirs of the ages, lords of the sea!
> Men of Devon, makers of the maps!
> Splendid fellows, capital chaps,
> > There's the foe!
> > Away we go!
> Good men, true men, follow me!

But nowadays it's different. The demagogue is
  proud
To explain to his supporters they're a miserable
  crowd,
And it seems that to electrify the British worker's
  blood
You address the man as dirt and you remind him he
  is mud,
Singing—

Wage-slaves! Yoke-fellows! Dolts and dupes!
Economic serfs and nincompoops!
Earth-worms, half-wits, capitalist pawns,
Jail-birds, jelly-fish, slum-scum, prawns,
Industrial cogs,
Poor fools and frogs,
Beggars and boobies—Vote for Me!

Our fathers found it wiser to throw very little dirt
At the persons they were seeking at the moment to
convert,
But now, if people argue when you say that black is
white,
You must kick them in the stomach till they see that
you are right,

Singing—

Parasites! Snobs! Shareholders! Rats!
Bosses! Bullies! Bloodsuckers! Bats!
Liberals, lap-dogs, black-legs, fools,
Company directors, capitalist tools,
Conservatives, stoats,
I want your votes—
Peers and parasites, Vote for Me!

SPORT SONG FOR SENTIMENTALISTS

[" There are so many foxes dug out and killed in this country by poachers that we are only too pleased to get them out ourselves and save them from such an ignoble death."—*From a M.F.H.'s letter.*

" If a fox goes to ground and you leave him the farmers set traps and he is caught and killed in a very much more painful way than dying fighting."—*From another ditto.*]

It's really remarkably pleasant
   To wander about in a wood
And kill an occasional pheasant,
   Provided the motive is good;
And one of the jolliest features
   Of slaying superfluous game
Is the thought that you're saving the creatures
   From a death of dishonour and shame.

Every bird has to die
By-and-by, by-and-by,
And they're lucky to die as they do,
For if they do not
They are probably shot
By someone who's not in " Who's Who";
And I give you my word
Any sensitive bird—
A point for our foolish reproachers—
Prefers his career
To be stopped by a peer
And not by unmannerly poachers.

446

Chorus

It's all for the sake of the bird, poor thing !
A point for the foolish reproacher !
And oft, I have heard,
On the face of the bird
A smile of serene
Satisfaction is seen—
To think that it wasn't a poacher !

Dumb creatures with me are a passion ;
  I've a special regard for the fox,
And I seek in my fatherly fashion
  To spare him excitement and shocks ;
The farmer is anxious to fill him
  With pellets, as farmers are wont,
And it's really a kindness to kill him,
  For he's certain to die if we don't.

Every fox has to die
By-and-by, by-and-by,
But what he can't bear is a gun ;
So we hunt him with dogs
Over meadows and bogs,
For that is his notion of fun.
And I vow and aver
That foxes prefer
To be killed, as it were, in their armour
By an aristocrat
In a shiny top-hat,
And not by an under-bred farmer.

CHORUS

It's all for the sake of the fox, poor thing!
He does like to die in his armour;
And oft on his face
At the end of the chase
A smile of serene
Satisfaction is seen—
To think that it wasn't a farmer!

THE WHITE WINE ELECTION

[" The one outstanding issue is the Eighteenth Amendment."
—*Daily Paper on the Presidential Election*, 1928.]

THERE'S a wild time now in the United States,
  In Alaska, Nebraska, Connecticut and Maine,
From Battery Point to the Golden Gates
  There's a hundred million Americans in pain.
    And what's it biting 'em?
    What's exciting 'em?
  Why do they make such lots of speeches?
    Is it European Pacts,
    Or the Immigration Acts,
  The size of fleets or the price of peaches,
    The Brotherhood of Man,
    Or a new Peace Plan?
Why do the papers rave and riot
  North and South of the Dixie Line?
Well, it's all about a difficult question of diet—
  Ought the Americans to drink white wine?

'Cos Bert says " Oughtn't " and Al says " Oughter "—
  And who'll be President of the United States?
Al wants wine and Bert whines " Water "—
  And who'll be President of the United States?
    Who'll be President, Al or Bert?
    Al thinks a little glass of Hock won't hurt.
      But Herbert has a shock
      If he sees a glass of Hock,

451

Graves or Chablis, Château Yquem,
And other pretty liquids I will not name,
For Bert don't like them and it seems a shame
(There's a lot to be said for Herbert Hoover,
But nobody could call him a gravity-remover).
  Anyhow, Hock
  Is the stumbling-block,
  Not ships or stock,
  Or the Monroe Doc.,
And north and south of the Dixie Line
They're all discussing how a man should dine—
Well, ought *Americans to drink white wine?*

Abraham Lincoln sits in the sky
  With good George Washington and one or two
    mates,
And "Abe," says Washington, "I can't think why
  There's all this noise in the United States."
    And Abraham says
    "When I was Pres.,
  Nobody could say we'd no ideels,
    But we didn't much mind
    How Americans dined,
  And we *never* had elections all about meals."
And George said, "Father told me it was rude
To talk in company about one's food,
And *I* never knew it mattered such a lot
If Americans drank white wine or not."

But Bert says "Oughtn't" and Al says "Oughter,"
  And who'll be President of the United States?

Al wants wine and Bert whines " Water,"
  And who'll be President of the United States?
    Who'll be President, Bert or Al?
    Bert thinks Rudesheimer's bad for Cal
    (There's a lot to be said for Herbert Hoover,
    But he's got a lot to learn as a gravity-remover).
      And if Al takes a knock
      Abandon hope of Hock,
      For Herbert has a shock
      If he sees a glass of Hock,
      And Hock, just Hock,
      Is the stumbling-block,
      Not ships or stock,
      Or the Monroe Doc.,
  So who'll be President of the United States?
Michigan, Missouri, Mississippi, Maryland,
Colorado, Kansas, Kentucky, Carolina,
Vermont, Virginia, Tennessee and Texas,
Arizona, Utah, Oregon, Nevada,
      Maine, Montana,
      Iowa, Indiana,
      And that's about all
      That I recall,
  But they're all discussing how a man should dine—
  Well, ought Americans to drink white wine?

PHARMACY WEEK

SONG-SLOGAN FOR A CHEMIST'S WINDOW

PAUSE, passer-by, and softly say,
Well, *am* I quite the thing today ?
The human race is far from strong,
And most of us have something wrong—
  Take It In Time !

Are you as well as you suppose ?
There is a pimple on your nose ;
And many a spot that size, my friend,
Becomes an abscess in the end—
  Take It In Time !

That little cough which you neglect
Will mean pneumonia, I expect ;
While Pyorrhœa lurks beneath
Four out of five of Britain's teeth—
  Take It In Time !

There are complaints which, if ignored,
Attack at last the spinal cord ;
And woe betide the child who scorns
Our cure for Chilblains, Chaps or Corns—
  Take It In Time !

You would not wish to see your wife
Dissected by the surgeon's knife ;
But that is what will happen if
She don't correct that tiresome sniff—
Take It In Time !

I knew a man whose horrid breath
Untimely drove him to his death ;
So I should gargle, Sir, with this
Extremely pleasant dentifrice—
Take It In Time !

One moment, Madam!   Try your weight.
Ah! seven stone.   You should be eight.
But we've a tonic, Ma'am, which may
Prevent your wasting quite away—
    Take It In Time!

Then 'tis impossible to tell
If the inside is working well;
You would be safer if you chewed
These little tablets after food—
    Take It In Time!

Gold is a curse, we all admit,
But you have not too much of it;
Why waste it then on Doctor's bills?
You have the pains and we the pills—
    Take Both In Time!

For Nervousness, Lassitude, Debility, Anæmia,
  Quinsy, Sciatica, Diseases of the Skin,
Rheumatism, Dandruff, Acute Septicæmia,
    The Colic and the Croup,
    The Shingles and the Stoop,
  Melancholy, Flatulence—walk right in!
Don't shut the door when the horse is stolen,
Don't sit and wonder why the gums are swollen,
We have the one and only proved panacea
For Sore Throat, Backache, Asthma, Pyorrhœa,
We sell Face-creams, Shaving-brushes, Soap,
Scents and Sponges, Hot-water Bottles, Hope,

We'll keep you thin,
Adiposity's a sin;
Or we'll keep you fat
If you fancy that.
Walk in !   Walk in !   One penny pill
Saves you a pound on the doctor's bill.
Something's wrong, though you don't look ill—
      Take It In Time !

TOO MUCH!

WELL, Mrs. Henn, and have you heard the latest?
　　Biggest bit of foolishness to date!
　　　Seems a millionaire
　　　With a lot of cash to spare
　　Has given fifty thousand to the State.

Just fancy, giving money to the Government!
　　Might as well have thrown it all away.
Fancy giving money to the Government
　　When you and me have got the rent to pay!
　　　Nobody can tell what men will do—
　　　Always breaking out with something new;
　　　Nothing can surprise me—can it you?
But fancy giving money to the Government!

When you think of all the milds and bitters
　　Fifty thousand Bradburys would buy!
　　　Think of all the fun
　　　You and me could have with *one*—
　　Isn't it enough to make you cry?

Well, fancy giving money to the Government!
　　Might as well have put it down the drain
Fancy giving money to the Government!
　　Nobody will see the stuff again.
　　　Well, they've no idea what money's for—
　　　Ten to one they'll start another war.
　　　I've heard a lot of silly things, but, Lor'!
Fancy giving money to the Government!

458

I know a man who thinks that he's a chicken,
  And you should hear him crowing when he lays!
    And then there's Uncle Fred
    Plays the cornet in his bed—
  Well, everyone has funny little ways :—

But fancy giving money to the Government !
  Many a man's locked up for less than that.
Fancy giving money to the Government,
  And me without a feather to me hat !
    Think of all the good he might have done !
    It's knocked the stuffing out of me, for one.
    Drat me, if I don't become a nun !
Well, fancy—
       giving—
           money—
              to the Government !

FAREWELL TO A LADY

(For Music)

I'll send thee no more roses, Eve,
　　Nor lilies gold and white,
But these with my true love receive,
　　And wear for me tonight.

So may they by thy touch be blessed,
　　And when we two must part,
I'll pluck one blossom from thy breast
　　And keep it next my heart.

For thou art still my dainty dove
　　And hast not any peer,
But I'll send no more roses, love,
　　Because they are too dear.

And oh! the daisy on the sward,
  The primrose by the lea,
The simple blooms I can afford
  Were never made for thee.

For thee the orchid paints his crest,
  For thee the eagles fly;
Thou wilt be clad in Nature's best,
  Or know the reason why.

So I'll forget thee if I can,
  And thou shalt have thy bliss,
For thou wilt find a dearer man,
  And I a cheaper Miss.

I'll send thee no more roses, Eve,
  Nor lilies gold and white,
But these with my true love receive,
  And wear for me tonight.

FAREWELL TO ANOTHER LADY

(For Jazz)

Good-bye, my love, good-bye, good-bye,
But dry, oh dry, that lovely eye!
    We must be brave,
    So do behave—
  The porter's staring so.
I'll be all right when you are gone,
I'll set my teeth and carry on.
    My dear, don't think
    I'll take to drink
  Or suicide—oh no!

    When you're away
      Don't think I'm moping;
    Life will be grey,
      But I'll keep hoping.
    When you're away
    I'll sigh and say,
      " She's not the only pearl " ;
    I'll cast my eye
    About and try
      To find another girl.

I do not think that you would say
We are unique in any way;
    Your eyes and feet
    Are very sweet,
  But so are millions more.
I have my points, I know, but then
There must be quite a lot of men
    No less refined
    And good and kind
  And easy to adore.

When you're away
   You'd best forget me,
And curse the day
   On which you met me.
Don't lose your grip,
That upper lip
   Keep rigid if you can;
Just cast your eye
About and try
   To find another man.

Ah, not again shall these lips touch—
But does that matter very much?
    It is a blow,
    But then, you know,
  Nobody cares but us;
The world will still go round and round,
And twenty bob still make a pound;
    My appetite
    Will be all right,
  So, darling, why the fuss?

When you're away,
  Don't think I'm moping;
With my dismay
  I'll keep on coping.
Just look about
And I've no doubt
  You'll land a landed Earl;
I'll cast my eye
About and try
  To find another girl.

NOTHING'S BEEN THE SAME

THANK you, Mrs. Thomas, and I don't mind if I do;
My dear, it seems an age since I was sitting here
with you.
I only hope you're better, dear, than what I am,
because—
Oh, well, we mustn't grumble, but I'm not the girl
I was.

Nothing's been the same since I took up with orange-
juice,
One always pays for foolishness, my dear—
Pains in the back and side,
My little bird has died,
And bilious—well, I couldn't tell you here!
Then we had the Frost, my dear, and then we had
the Flood,
And Bert's been quite a martyr to suppression of
the blood.
Oranges? I tell you, dear, with me their name is mud—
So what about a little drop of beer?

A tumbler night and morning! Well, I'd just as
soon have ink;
It's what you're bred and born to is the safest, don't
you think?
And don't you let 'em talk you round with this
reducing stuff—
There used to be too much of me, and now there's
not enough.

466

Nothing's been the same since I took up with orange-
    juice;
  It never does to shock the system, dear:
      My temper's kind of terse,
      The weather's worse and worse,
  And the Government is acting very queer.
Well, that's what comes of tampering with Providence,
    you see;
It's oranges for animals, but hops for you and me:
I wouldn't touch another if I had my private tree—
  But what about a nice drop of beer?

I've lost my loving-kindness, dear, I've lost my
self-control,
And Mabel thinks that what I've got is jaundice
on the soul;
You'd be surprised—this morning I had words
with Mrs. Drew,
And many of them words, my dear, I didn't know
I *knew!*

*Nothing's been the same since I took up with orange-
    juice,*
  The slightest thing excites me now, my dear;
      I used to live and let,
      But now I seem to get
  A nasty sort of itch to interfere.

I'm not the Christian woman what I used to be before;
*Poor Bert's took up with betting, dear, and I've begun
    to snore;*
*Oranges?   If it's for me, they needn't grow no more—
    But what about a healthy drop of beer?*

LINES FOR A WORTHY PERSON WHO HAS DRIFTED BY ACCIDENT INTO A CHELSEA REVEL

IT is a very curious fact
That those who write or paint or act,
　　Compose or etch
　　Or sculp or sketch,
　Or practise things like pottery,
Have not got consciences like us,
Are frankly not monogamous;
　　Their moral tone
　　Is all their own,
　Their love-affairs a lottery.
It's hard to say why writing verse
Should terminate in drink or worse,
　　Why flutes and harps
　　And flats and sharps
　Should lead to indiscretions;
But if you read the Poets' Lives
You'll find the number of their wives
　　In fact exceeds
　　The normal needs
　Of almost all professions.
As my poor father used to say
　　In 1863,
Once people start on all this Art
　　Goodbye, moralitee!
And what my father used to say
　　Is good enough for me.

469　　　　　16 *

Oh, may no little child of mine
Compose or model, draw, design,
　　And sit at ease
　　On people's knees,
　With other odious habits!
See what eccentric things they wear,
Observe their odd un-English hair—
　　The women bald,
　　The men (so-called)
　As thickly furred as rabbits!
Not these the kind of people who
Were prominent at Waterloo,
　　Not this the stock
　　Which stood the shock
　When Kaiser picked his quarrel.
Let Dagoes paint and write and sing,
But Art is not an English thing;
　　Better be pure
　　And die obscure
　Than famous but immoral!

As my poor father used to say
　　In 1863,
Once people start on all this Art
　　Farewell, monogamee!
And what my father used to say,
And what my father used to say,
　　Is good enough for me.

And shall we let this canker stick
Inside the body politic?

Oh, let us take
Some steps to make
Our messy nation cleaner !
The whole is greater than the part,
We should at once prohibit Art,
Let Music be
A felony
And Verse a misdemeanour ;
Let long-haired gentlemen who draw
Be segregated by the law,
And every bard
Do six months' hard
Who lyrically twaddles,
But licences be issued to
A few selected curates, who
Shall fashion odes
In serious modes
On statutory models.

As my poor father used to say
In 1863,
Once people start on all this Art
Farewell, moralitee !
And what my father used to say,
And what my father used to say,
And what my father used to say,
Is good enough for me.

NOTE ON THE WRITING OF FRENCH POETRY

The "Chanson du Lizard," which follows, should have a Message for all cruising yachtsmen, though its particular appeal must be to the passengers and crew of the yacht *Lizard*. It may have no point for others, but I do not care; I print it here because I am proud of my French verse, and I am proud of that because I know very little French. Also, I wish to show up the French poets. I have discovered that the writing of French verse is much easier than the writing of English verse (or French prose); and, given a thorough knowledge of the French language, it must be child's play. Rhymes are more plentiful (especially in the department of love), and the most bald and banal statement has a kind of spurious distinction when put into French. I made the discovery when I audaciously burst into French lyrics for Sir Nigel Playfair's production of "La Vie Parisienne." Take, for example, the stanza:

> "Paris, c'est l'amour
> Et l'alimentation,
> Manger toujours
> Et toujours la passion—
> Meals and misses
> Bocks and blisses,
> Cooking and kisses—
> Ça c'est Paris."

The first four lines are, so they tell me, profoundly true; but also they seem to me to have a poetical ring which the assertion contained in them scarcely deserves. The succeeding lines, in which the squalid theme is restated in brutal English, are technically as good, but they do not *sound* so good.

Take, again, the final chorus :

> " À quoi bon
> L'ambition?
> Ça ne vaut pas la pein-e.
> Donnez moi
> Baiser—ma foi,
> Je suis roi et rein-e !
>
> Jamais la jeuness-e
> Sera de retour ;
> Mort à la tristess-e,
> Et viv-e l'amour !"

Here the thought is not, perhaps, startlingly original, and some of the French may be erroneous ; but the sound is fine. The same bare thought, neatly expressed in English verse, would not have the same effect. But continental poets have been building up a reputation on this kind of thing for centuries. Given a knowledge of French, a light heart, and a generous sprinkling of the word "amour," I believe that anyone could do it. If I am wrong, show me a French poet who could write a passable lyric in English. If I am right, it follows that some of our serious English poets, who show a strange incapacity for metrical composition in their own tongue, might be well advised to express themselves in the easier language of the French.

I write all my French poetry without aid except a Handy Dictionary ; but I asked a French girl to "vet" my lyrics for this production.   She could speak no English and I very little French, and since we were almost unable to converse in French prose, the discussion of my French verse was difficult.   She found several dreadful wrong genders (which took me four or five days to correct), but she said that my lyrics were "très spirituel"; and I think she was right.

CHANSON DU LIZARD

"À Terre Nous Allons!"

Story of the Poem.—Yacht " Lizard " is cruising along coasts of Brittany. Owner's Wife detests ocean, and yacht, like most yachts, spends more time in harbour than at sea. When in harbour, Owner, who is a Brigadier-General, has strange passion for visiting remote churches and ruins on hot afternoons. Owner's Wife prefers "*rester tranquille*" in " Lizard." Owner's Wife detests expeditions and ruins, especially the large stones left about the countryside by Druids. And see the " Note on the Writing of French Poetry."

> *Allons, allons un peu plus loin !*
> *Il faut trouver un joli coin*
> *Où l'Océan ne troubl-e[1] point—*
> *Ha, ha ! le brav-e " Lizard "!*

> Les vag-ues et les vents,
> Les rochers et les îl-es,
> Sont toujours évidents—
> Mon Dieu ! c'est difficil-e ![2]

[1] For the benefit of those not accustomed to sing in French, I have emphasized with hyphens the strange French custom of sounding final " e." When inconvenient it is not done. So French.

[2] Whenever a Breton fisherman is asked for information about channels, etc., he replies " C'est assez difficile," and goes away.

Le Général préfèr-e
Regarder les pierr-es,[1]
Allons, allons à terr-e,
   À terr-e nous allons !

Allons, allons ! un peu plus loin,
De port à port, de coin à coin,
Où l'Océan ne troubl-e point—
   Ha, ha ! le brav-e " Lizard "!

Qu'est-il de plus sublim-e
   Que d'aller à la voil-e—
La vi-e maritim-e,
   Les phar-es, les étoil-es ?
Moi-mêm-e, je préfèr-e
M'asseoin avec mon verr-e
Mais il n'y a plus de bièr-e—
   À terr-e nous allons

Allons, allons un peu plus loin,
Car je connais un joli coin,
Où l'Océan ne troubl-e point
   Ha, ha ! le brav-e " Lizard "!

Mon brav-e Général
   Veut s'promener à l'Ouessant,
Par un petit chenal
   Qui est tres intéressant ;

---

[1] *I.e.*, Les dolmens, menhirs, cromlechs, etc., qui se trouvent en Bretagne et excitent l'Owner formidablement, mais pas sa famille : ni moi non plus.

Mais sa femm-e préfer-e
Rester dans la rivièr-e;
Nous restons donc à terr-e,
   À terr-e nous restons!

Demain, peut-être, un peu plus loin!
Mais je connais un joli coin
Où l'Océan ne troubl-e point—
   Ha, ha! le brav-e " Lizard "!

Il n'y a pas assez d'eau,[1]
   Mais il y a trop de vent,
Allons à Concarneau!
   C'est mieux que l'Océan.
Il y a une forte odeur,
De poissons et d'pêcheurs,
Elle ne nous fait pas peur,
   À terr-e nous allons!

Allons, demain, un peu plus loin!
Quel' senteur a ce joli coin!
Mais il est tranquille, néanmoins—
   Ha, ha! le brav-e " Lizard "!

Marchons aux magasins![2]
   Nous n'avons plus de poissons,
Nous n'avons plus de vin,
   Nous n'avons plus de croissants;[3]

[1] After anchor has been dropped in a strange tidal harbour question is always put to a local fisherman, " Il y a assez d'eau?" Answer is always " Non."

[2] Shopping is the only part of yachting which really matters. When no other excuse for seeking harbour, Owner's Wife says, " We have no more bread," and that settles it.

[3] Rime effrayante? C'est vrai. Mais que voulez-vous?

Nous n'avons plus de glac-e,
Voilà un port en fac-e,
Nous débarquons en mass-e,
La Terr-e, je t'embrass-e,
   Et au revoir, La Mer !

Allons, allons un peu plus loin,
Car je connais un joli coin,
Où l'Océan ne troubl-e point—
   Ha, ha ! le brav-e " Lizard "!

À terr-e nous allons,
   Riez, mon Aristide ![1]
Et nous, nous visitons
   Les dolmens des Druid-es.
La Mer est vaste et vid-e ;
Je n'aime pas les Druid-es,
Mais ils sont plus solid-es—
   À terr-e nous allons !

Allons, allons, un peu plus loin,
Il faut trouver un joli coin
Où l'Océan ne troubl-e point,
   Ha, ha ! le brav-e " Lizard "!

Au brav-e petit bateau
   Je lèv-e donc mon verr-e !
Au Général de l'eau,
   Aux enfants et leur mèr-e.
Aussi à l'équipag-e[2]

[1] French cook, acquired at Brest. Very fortunate, as few rhymes to Druides.
[2] Crew.

Bonne chance et bon voyag-e !
Adieu, et soyez sag-es,
Évitez les naufrag-es,
Surveillez les nuag-es,
Tenez-vous à la plag-e,
   À la plag-e tenez.

Allez plus loin, mais ayez soin !
Chers matelots, il y a peu de coins
Où l'Océan ne troubl-e point—
   Ha, ha ! le brav-e " Lizard " !

BRIEF LECTURE TO A SERIOUS POET

THE writers of light verse have a good title to lecture the serious poets at the present time. It has never been clear to us why light verse, however good, should be regarded as inferior to " serious " poetry, however bad. "Slim volumes" of careless undergraduate gush, formless and, to most minds, meaningless, have always received much more attention from the literary papers than the works of masters of the lighter art, which are generally described as "these gay pages," or "joyous doggerel." The technique (if any) of the serious lads is analyzed with reverent solemnity : but the technique of Mr. Belloc or Mr. Chesterton or Mr. J. C. Squire (in their lighter moods), of Sir Owen Seaman, Mr. A. A. Milne, Mr. E. V. Knox, or Mr. Harry Graham, has never, so far as I know, been mentioned in public, though it is the fruit of immense ability and labour. It is taken for granted ; probably the reviewer does not realize it is there. It is just as well that reviewers should remain silent on matters which they do not understand ; but this is one illustration of the first main theme of my lecture, which is the Under-Valuation of Light or Comic Poetry. It is not sufficiently esteemed as a difficult and important form of literary art. A Gray can make a reputation with a single Elegy : but a Gilbert has to write twelve Operas, and even then he is not considered to matter so much as Mr. Gray.

This was reasonable enough while the standard of serious poetry was high. We are accustomed to the absurd old notion, first put about by Aristotle, that " tragedy is superior to comedy," which means in these days that a mediocre lament is better than a good laugh. But things have changed. The Comic Muse of this country is in very fine fettle. You will not think so, it is true, if you go to a contemporary musical comedy and hear the incompetent drivel which passes for " lyrics " in most of them, and is accepted without protest, apparently, by the British race, who, having produced Gay and Sheridan and Gilbert, ought to know better. But that is another story, and a long one : the History of the Influence of American Music on English Verse has still to be written. The managers (with one exception) do not want songs now : they want " dance-numbers " : and " dance-numbers " want Jazz : and Jazz music, so far as it wants words at all, wants words without form or substance, rhythm or rhyme. And so we hear " lyrics " of this kind :

> " To me you seem the cream of perfection,
>   You are so intensely alive,
>   I like your style,
>   You are the cream in my coffee,
>   O Baby, sincerely,
>   I love you dearly—
>   And say !
>   I know a parson
>   Who's out of work today."

I have just composed those lines : and I see now they are too good. It is almost impossible to parody the dance-songs (chiefly American) which are whined, whispered, or wheezed on the stage, screen, or gramophone today.   But if we forget the stage and screen (as, alas! we must), the original assertion stands.   For very many years we have had giants in this field of writing.   The men I have named already (and one or two others) can do the thing as well and as easily as Gilbert (though they have not his theatrical gifts and opportunities), and twenty times as well as Gay.   Mr. Belloc and Mr. Chesterton are serious poets (and several other things as well) : but for their light and comic verse alone they deserve the largest laurels the country can provide. Compared with Mr. Belloc, Mr. Gay is a novice at the game.   This is perhaps the one department of writing in which, as a nation, we can confidently claim that we have advanced, that we are better than our forefathers.

I do not know whether our literary pundits will admit this claim : I fancy they have never considered it, being obsessed by the idea that only the serious gentlemen matter.   But will they claim that the serious poets are better than their forefathers ?

It is not for me to answer that question.   I would not venture to criticize even my contemporaries in their own field of labour.   The output does not seem, to an outsider, to be large : but I know that the market is not what it was.   Perhaps for that reason, in a sort of despair, they have in recent times increasingly trespassed on our domain : one or two have even ventured to be funny.   And here, at last, is our title to lecture them.

We welcome the invaders (I name no names) provided only that they do not let our standards of workmanship down: they may blackleg, but they must observe the rules of the craft. And this, I am sorry to say, they do not do. My contemporaries, the post-war serious poets, are very fine fellows, and have done much fine work. But (now that they have their bouquets) I hope they will admit that, broadly speaking, their distinctive achievement has been their bold, rebellious abandonment of formal correctitude. We know the reasons for that. Inspiration in these wild times comes spouting up with such a force and flow that the narrow formalities of Mr. Keats and others cannot contain it. You cannot make the fierce geysers of New Zealand perform like the fountains of Trafalgar Square. You cannot compress a volcano into a suburban grate. And you cannot enclose a modern poet in rhyming schemes and metrical rules. The verses burst themselves, the rhymes take charge: lines which should have had eight feet swell up uncontrollably to ten or twelve; " parrot " in an ecstasy rhymes itself with " spirit," odd monosyllabic lines fly out like sparks, and at last, as like as not, both rhyme and metre are blown to the winds, and we get a page or two of pure poetry, unconfined by either. What of that ? Rhyme was made for the poet, not the poet for the rhyme. Why should not " haddock " rhyme with " buttock " or " Médoc " ? It is the spirit, not the letter, that matters. A poem is not a tennis-court, to be marked out in rectangles. Does the wild honeysuckle grow in the geranium-bed ? It does not.

Yes, my serious friend, we know all that. It is not, as I have heard men say, incompetence or laziness that makes the lines of your tennis-court wriggle and wander so: it is inspiration, or modernity, or the revolt of youth against the older generation; or you are making experiments in word-patterns, or this or that. If you chose, you could find an exact rhyme for "haddock"; but exact rhymes are "*vieux jeu*", Georgian, Royal-Academical; the tennis-courts of revolting youth are no more rectangular; the service-court is a rhomboid, and the side-lines wander in graceful but rebellious curves across the flower-beds and back. And a nasty slap in the face for the older generation it is.

Yes, my friend, we know all that. And so long as you confine yourself to serious poetry you may (as they vulgarly say) get away with it. But if you are going to be funny, or even light, it will not do. It is the old story. The parson may provoke us to yawns with impunity, but the comedian must hold his audience all the time. This is a very hard school of writing. If *we* set out light-heartedly on a difficult rhyming scheme we must go on with it, and no explosive inspiration, revolts of youth and what-not, will excuse us if we fail. But you serious lads come blustering in and think you can do what you like. You bespatter your pages with dreadful slovenly rhymes, and when we complain, you say that you did it—"for fun"! Nonsense! Now and then we may commit a bad rhyme "for fun"; but if you do it in every stanza the defence wears thin. Then you tell us you are "in the Byronic tradition". That does not impress us: we are a long way ahead of Byron in this department, and you must be bound by our standards, not his. If you do not, you will presently be complaining that the market in comic verse is a poor one. It is not a matter of narrow pedantry, but of professional honesty. If you announce that you are going to write a poem in long stanzas with numerous rhymes you create a definite expectation in the reader. And if you continually fail to find the right rhyme, because the task is too difficult or laborious, you disappoint and defraud the reader. He may forgive you in your own department, but he will not in ours. It would be a very good exercise for you, my young, rebellious, bubbly friend, to write a series of poems in some strict form, the Ballade, the Sonnet, or the Limerick, perhaps the most difficult of all (queer, by the way, that the amateur nearly always selects that form!). And I would advise you, before you begin, to study humbly the works of Mr. Belloc, grave and gay. There you will find that perfection of form which we old-fashioned fellows still regard as valuable. There is no sense of strain or confinement: everything the writer wishes to say is said: but every word and every rhyme is as precisely fitted into its place as are the stones of an arch. (But perhaps you dislike the pedantic formality of arches, would prefer to have the stones protruding untidily here and there, to express the revolt of youth.) It looks easy, as Mr. Belloc does it, but it is very hard work.

In this "slim volume" you will find much to repel you, a low moral tone, a flippant attitude to serious

problems, some feeble efforts for fun, and almost no
attempt to elevate or instruct.   But none of the
gross faults you will find can be put down, I think,
to lack of care, conscience, or industry.   I will not
tell you how many days of hard labour each wretched
little piece demanded : you would say it was time
wasted, and the information would not interest anybody else.   I only mention the odious topic of work
because, to be quite frank at last, my friend, I suspect,
in spite of all your fine defences, the real truth is
that you serious lads are rather *lazy*.

One reason, my friend, why I want you to be a
little less modern and sprawly and careless is that I
hope you will write us some *songs*.   We have a
wealth of poets, yet we produce almost nothing in
the way of native song or light opera.   Surely the
English race has not said its last word in the line of
lyric drama.   You, with your poetical gifts, fine
thoughts and modern fancies, might open a new
vein.   But you will have to be more direct and
singable and understandable : and of, course, you
will have to work.   Don't tell me there are no good
composers—there are rows of them.   I cannot
promise that you will receive much immediate en-
couragement from the London managers (one, again,
excepted).   But that should not deter a bold boy like
you.   Even Jazz will have its day, and the English
lyric will be heard again.   Sit down now, and write
" ACT ONE."

PRINTED IN GREAT BRITAIN BY
BILLING AND SONS LIMITED,
GUILDFORD AND ESHER